PROGRAM MANUAL

Support for Students Exposed to Trauma: The SSET Program

Group Leader Training Manual, Lesson Plans, and Lesson Materials and Worksheets

Lisa H. Jaycox • Audra K. Langley • Kristin L. Dean

Sponsored by the National Institute of Mental Health

RAND HEALTH

This work was sponsored by the National Institute of Mental Health under contract No. MH072591. The research was conducted in RAND Health.

Library of Congress Cataloging-in-Publication Data is available for this publication.

978-0-8330-4732-8

Published 2009 by the RAND Corporation
1776 Main Street, P.O. Box 2138, Santa Monica, CA 90407-2138
1200 South Hayes Street, Arlington, VA 22202-5050
4570 Fifth Avenue, Suite 600, Pittsburgh, PA 15213-2665
RAND URL: http://www.rand.org/
To order RAND documents or to obtain additional information, contact
Distribution Services: Telephone: (310) 451-7002;
Fax: (310) 451-6915; Email: order@rand.org

Preface

These materials were adapted from a manualized group program called the Cognitive-Behavioral Intervention for Trauma in Schools, or CBITS, which was developed and initially evaluated in the Los Angeles Unified School District. That program was developed for use by school-based mental health professionals, whereas the Support for Students Exposed to Trauma (SSET) program, the subject of this book, can be used by any school personnel with the time and interest to work with students affected by trauma.

To adapt and develop the SSET program for teachers and school counselors, we consulted with school and mental health experts, conducted focus groups with school staff and parents, and used their feedback to develop the program and pilot test it in two Los Angeles Unified School District middle schools. Results of the pilot test were promising, showing that teachers and school counselors were able to deliver the program as desired, that students and parents were satisfied with the support groups, and that children showed small improvements in their distress symptoms.[1]

We thank the many individuals who contributed to this project: Bradley Stein, Marleen Wong, Stefanie Stern, Steven Evans, Phyllis Ellickson, Sheryl Kataoka, Barbara Colwell, Roberta Bernstein, Pia Escudero, Fernando Cadavid, Suzanne Blake, Daryl Narimatsu, Patricia Fuentes-Gamboa, Yvette Landeros, Lajuana Worship, Maria Sanchez, Kathy Scott, Rachel Braude, Brian Spencer, Kris Evans, Carla Heiland, Benin Williams, Jonathan Brown, Windy Wilkins, and the many parents and students who helped us develop this manual.

This book has three parts: a training manual for SSET leaders and other implementers, the SSET lesson plans, and the SSET lesson materials and worksheets that accompany each lesson. The training manual can be read first, followed by each lesson plan and its accompanying materials as they are referenced in the plan. The materials and worksheets are reproducible for use when implementing the SSET program. They can be either photocopied directly from this book or printed out directly from the RAND Corporation's Web site at http://www.rand.org/publications/TR-675.

This work was sponsored by the National Institute of Mental Health under contract No. MH072591. The research was conducted in RAND Health, a division of the RAND Corporation. A profile of RAND Health, abstracts of its publications, and ordering information can be found at www.rand.org/health.

---

[1] Jaycox, L. H., Langley, A. K., Stein, B. D., Wong, M., Sharma, P., Scott, M., Schonlau, M. (2009). Support for Students Exposed to Trauma: A Pilot Study. School Mental Health. Published online on March 21, 2009.

Contents

Glossary of Terms

Brainstorming

The act of eliciting any idea that pops into one's head that may be relevant to the situation. Should include all thoughts without judgment.

Distraction

The act of engaging in one behavior to take one's mind off another. May be used to help one endure anxiety during an exposure or as an option for managing a difficult social situation. Examples of distraction include listening to music, talking to a friend, playing a video game, thinking about something else, and watching TV or a movie.

Fear Thermometer

A tool for describing levels of negative feelings (e.g., fear, anxiety, worry, nervousness, upset) on a scale from 0 to 10, where 0 is "no problem at all; feeling good," and 10 is "feeling maxed out; the worst." Provides a common language for group members to describe and monitor their feelings; allows the group leader to gain insight into and monitor changes in an individual's anxiety levels.

Helpful thoughts

Thoughts that are based on a realistic assessment of the situation, including checking the objective facts, conducting an assessment of the most reasonable explanation, and reviewing the history of similar occurrences.

Positive images

Ideas or mental pictures that are associated with feelings of happiness, contentment, tranquility, calm, and relaxation. Individuals may imagine themselves in a setting or situation that conjures these emotions, or they may simply imagine a picture that reminds them of this state of relaxation.

Problem solving

The act of figuring out ways to best manage difficult situations. Includes brainstorming solutions, evaluating all proposed options, implementing the strategy deemed best to reach individual goal while maintaining the safety of all involved, and limiting negative associated consequences.

Relaxation	Exercise(s) directed at reducing physiological arousal/tension. May include deep breathing, progressive muscle tensing and relaxing, and positive visual imagery.
Social support	Care provided to an individual by another person (e.g., a family member, a friend, a neighbor, a teacher).
SSET	Support for Students Exposed to Trauma.
Thought stopping	The deliberate act of willing oneself to stop a current thought. Typically done by visualizing a stop sign, saying "Stop!" out loud or to oneself, or doing something else that serves as a cue to stop the thought (such as snapping a rubber band or banging one's hand on a table, book, or desk).
Trauma narrative	An individual's relating of the story of his or her traumatic experience. A written, verbal, or pictorial expression of the occurrences that comprised one's traumatic event.
Trauma/traumatic event	An event that is sudden and frightening and that poses a threat of injury or death to oneself or others. Usually makes an individual feel terrified, horrified, or helpless when it is happening.
Unrealistic thoughts	Thoughts that are not based on available objective evidence and may not be reasonable for the situation or context.

GROUP LEADER TRAINING MANUAL

Audra K. Langley
Lisa H. Jaycox
Kristin L. Dean

Prevalence and Impact of Exposure to Violence

Exposure to community and interpersonal violence is a public health crisis and adversely affects many children in our country and in our communities. A national study of 7–12th graders revealed that

- 12 percent of youth had a knife or gun pulled on them in the past year
- 5 percent had been stabbed or cut
- 1.5 percent had been shot at.[1]

There are some children who are at **greater risk for violence**, including

- boys
- older children
- children with early behavioral problems
- youth living in urban areas
- children with lower socioeconomic status.[2]

Following direct exposure to or after personally witnessing a traumatic event, many children experience symptoms of a disorder called ***Post-Traumatic Stress Disorder*** (PTSD); a substantial minority of these children show clinical levels of PTSD. Symptoms include

- re-experiencing the traumatic event (i.e., having flashbacks and/or intrusive thoughts about the event, having nightmares, becoming upset by exposure to reminders of the event)
- physiological hyperarousal (i.e., feeling startled more easily, being on guard for danger, getting angry/irritated easily, having trouble sleeping, poor concentration)
- avoidance/numbing (i.e., trying to avoid thoughts, people, and other reminders of the trauma; feeling numb emotionally; not remembering all of what happened).

In addition to PTSD, exposure to violence is also associated with **depression, behavioral problems, substance abuse, and poor school performance** in children. Among adolescents, approximately 6 percent of boys and 4 percent of girls meet clinical criteria for a diagnosis of PTSD. These rates are much higher for youth in urban areas, where they range from 24 percent to 67 percent. Moreover, 75 percent of youth with PTSD have additional mental health problems.

---

[1] Gutterman, N. B., Hahm, H. C., & Cameron, M. (2002). Adolescent victimization and subsequent use of mental health counseling services. Journal of Adolescent Health, 30(5): 336–345.

[2] Schwab-Stone, M., Chen, C., Greenberger, E., Silver, D., Lichtman, J., & Voyce, C. (1999). No Safe Haven II: The effects of violence exposure on urban youth. Journal of the American Academy of Child & Adolescent Psychiatry, 38(4), 359–367.

What Is SSET?

Support for Students Exposed to Trauma (SSET) is a series of ten support groups that use a structured approach to reduce distress resulting from exposure to violence. It includes a wide variety of skill-building techniques. These techniques are geared toward changing maladaptive thoughts (i.e., toward challenging negative thinking, stopping automatic negative thoughts, distracting from negative patterns of thinking) and promoting positive behaviors (i.e., improving social skills, increasing pleasant activities, decreasing avoidance of difficult situations or thoughts).

Each lesson follows a similar format:

- **Lessons are structured.** The agenda set for each lesson includes an independent practice review, teaching new skills or practicing other skills, and an independent practice assignment.
- **Lessons rely on collaboration between the group leader and the students.** The group leader acts as a "coach" to help the students develop new skills and find ways to practice them effectively.
- **Lessons emphasize the practice of new techniques during lessons and between lessons.** Independent practice assignments are assigned between lessons and are important for consolidating skills learned in group.
- **The SSET program is intended to be time-limited.** Groups encompass ten 1-hour meetings. The goal is to enable the students to continue practice on their own after the group ends.

What Problems Are Addressed by SSET?

This program is intended for use with groups of students who have experienced significant traumatic experiences and are suffering from symptoms of **PTSD, including re-experiencing the trauma, physiological hyperarousal, and numbing or avoidance.** Since low mood, anxiety or nervousness, and impulsive or angry behavior often accompany symptoms of PTSD, many of the techniques are targeted toward those problems as well. Thus, the following types of problems are addressed:

- anxiety or nervousness
- withdrawal or isolation
- low mood
- acting out in school
- impulsive or risky behavior.

What Problems Are *Not* Intended to Be Addressed by SSET?

The SSET program is not intended for use with

- students in crisis who need an immediate referral to counseling
- students with severe behavior problems that would make it hard for them to participate in a support group without disrupting it
- students with severe cognitive limitations that put them below the 4th-grade level in reading comprehension
- students whose primary problem is child abuse. (See "Working with Students Who Have Been Multiply Traumatized or Abused," pp. 27–28.)

Who Implements SSET?

SSET is designed to be implemented by teachers or school counselors who have an interest in the mental health of their students and have good rapport with their students. In addition to the implementer, it is important to have support from the school principal and other staff, who will need to be able to understand the reason for the groups, the plan for implementation, and how confidentiality will be handled. A very important piece of the SSET planning is forming an ongoing relationship with a clinician who can provide clinical backup support for the groups at the following times: at the beginning when students are identified for SSET, as the program is implemented in case any problems emerge, and at the end to ensure continuity for students who need additional support. Clinicians can be on staff at the school (e.g., a school-based social worker), available through the district (e.g., a psychologist or social worker at the district level), or contractually arranged with a community provider.

What Age Groups Benefit from SSET?

This program was designed for use in middle school (ages 10–14). It may be useful for younger students (down to grade 4) or older students (up to grade 9), but has not been used in those age groups to date.

What Skills Are Taught by SSET?

An outline of the new concepts taught in each lesson is provided in Table 1 on the next page.

Table 1—Lesson Outline

Lesson Number	Lesson Content
One	Introduction
Two	Common reactions to trauma and strategies for relaxation
Three	Thoughts and feelings
Four	Helpful thinking
Five	Facing your fears
Six	Trauma narrative, part one
Seven	Trauma narrative, part two
Eight	Problem solving
Nine	Practice with social problems and the Hot Seat
Ten	Planning for the future and graduation

Group Format and Management

Student support groups are formatted to last approximately one hour. The usual format is to convene groups of identified students during the school day, preferably during a nonacademic period. Groups can also be held after school if such obstacles as transportation concerns can be addressed. Groups are usually held once per week. In some groups, it is helpful to write an outline of the lesson's activities on the chalkboard at the beginning of the lesson. It may also be useful to develop a point system to increase participation in activities. The group members who complete the most activities can be rewarded, or incentives for activities participation can be provided throughout the program. Any such group-management techniques can be implemented to augment group participation and compliance.

Materials Needed

Notebooks containing the program handouts should be created for the participants, and extra copies should be made in case students lose or misplace their notebooks. For each lesson, have a chalkboard or large writing pad and extra copies of the relevant worksheets. Special materials required for each lesson are identified in the Teacher Preparation section of each lesson in the Lesson Plans section. Depending on the time of the intervention, it could be important to provide a snack or drinks for the participants.

Parent Participation

Parents are not involved in the group itself but should be engaged as much as possible through telephone contact. The first phone call to parents should occur at the beginning of SSET, preferably before the group lessons begin, but at the latest before Lesson Two. During this call, describe common reactions to stress or trauma, explain SSET and its procedures, and enlist parental help with activity assignments and group attendance. Subsequent phone calls can be made as needed. They may prove helpful in preparation for the real-life exposure activities in Lesson Five and can also be used to review a student's progress and suggest additional treatment, if necessary.

Confidentiality

Unlike many other activities at school, the SSET groups are designed to be confidential. **This means that what is shared in group stays in group, and even the group leader is expected to keep information about students confidential or private.** There are two exceptions to this rule:

1. If you determine that a student might be harmed or might harm others, you will need to follow school protocols to protect the student or others. (For example, if the student is having a medical emergency, or if he or she tells you about suicidal intent.)
2. If the student tells you about child abuse, you must follow school protocols and inform the study team as required by law.

The following types of information are expected to be kept **confidential**:

- scores on or responses to the screener measures
  - Only summary information can be shared with parents at the beginning of the group in order to explain the group's purpose. Otherwise, the overall scores or responses of students to any of the items on the screener measures are private.
- scores on or responses to any of the assessments
  - If you help to collect the assessments, remember that these are private.
- drawings or stories or worksheets generated as part of the group
  - All group materials should be stored and locked. They should not be shown to anyone outside of the group.
- student's experiences or statements made in group that they have not discussed in public settings
  - For example, some students may talk freely about their experiences in the hallways and classrooms, and if they do that in front of you, you are not bound to keep that information private. But if they are only talking about their experiences in the SSET group, or you are not sure, then you need to keep their experiences and statements private.
- inclusion in the group, beyond the need for others to know for logistic purposes

– For example, you may need to tell another teacher that the student is in group in order for the student to be released to you, but you do not need to tell anyone else that the student is participating in the group.

> **Note**
>
> If someone asks you for information about a student in your SSET group, *do not give it out* until you discuss it with the project team.

Goals and Theory of SSET

Goals

The goals of the SSET program are to

- reduce symptoms of PTSD and other related problems
- build resilience
- build peer and parent support.

Each of these goals needs to be tailored to the individual student. A review of the screening questionnaire will help to show student strengths and weaknesses and help this planning process.

The initial goal of SSET, then, is to **decrease the PTSD, depression, and general anxiety symptoms that are interfering with each student's functioning**. For example, if a student who has undergone a traumatic event is experiencing intrusive thoughts of the event, difficulty sleeping, general anxiety, poor concentration, negative ideas about himself or herself, irritability, and low mood, it is fairly clear that the event is interfering in his or her daily life. School performance, family and social relationships, and social activities may all be negatively affected by these symptoms. SSET aims to give students skills that help **decrease these symptoms and improve their functioning** at home, at school, and with friends.

Another goal of SSET is to assist students in maximizing the benefit of their existing coping skills and in building helpful new life skills in order to cope with the traumatic events they have encountered. This enables students to gain a sense of coping ability and mastery over managing their internal symptoms and their environments. As youth become practiced at various coping skills, they are then **equipped with a "toolkit"** from which they can pull various strategies to apply to different situations or elements of the event or issue they are facing.

A final goal of SSET is to **increase levels of peer and parent support**. SSET is an opportunity for youth to share information about their experiences with violence, trauma, or stress in a very supported way. It is also essential to create a foundation for support from peers and family members that will extend outside of the group. Participation in the group itself allows a common bond to develop between peer participants that oftentimes extends outside of the group. Moreover, some of the group content aims to give students skills for being able to appropriately share their experiences with violence, trauma, or stress with trusted others outside of the group (including trusted friends, family members or caregivers, teachers, and/or other adults). A common theme running though the SSET program is opening and strengthening

11

lines of understanding and communication between parents or caregivers and their children. This is done through education and take-home practice assignments.

SSET, then, aims to target both (1) the symptoms that students are presenting that are related to PTSD, depression, and behavioral problems and (2) the students' level of functioning at school, socially, and within their families. It is also aimed at building buffers, such as coping skills and peer and parent support, to enable students to deal with past and future events.

The Theory Behind SSET

At a basic level, the theory behind this type of program is that thoughts, feelings, and behaviors are closely related and can affect each other. This relationship is expressed in Figure 1.

Figure 1—Stress/Trauma/Violence Triangle

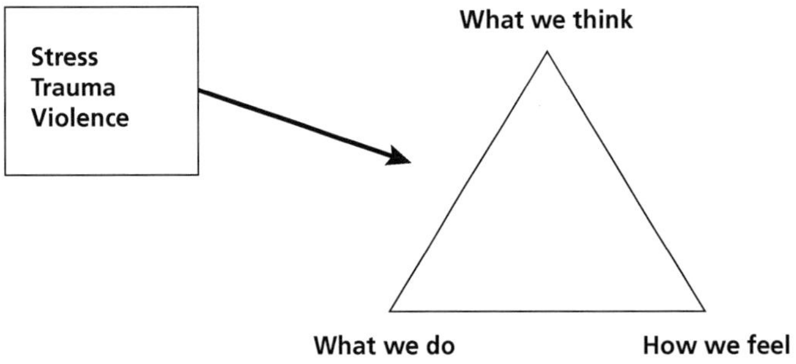

For example, suppose that as you are driving to work you encounter a lot of traffic.

Stress: Traffic on the way to work.

If you are thinking something positive or neutral about a situation, you will likely be feeling a positive emotion and only a little arousal in your body. You will behave accordingly.

Thoughts: "This should be fine. I'm good at handling this."

Feelings: Content, relaxed.

Actions: Driving normally.

On the other hand, if you are thinking negative things about a situation and negative emotions and physical feelings of anxiety arise, you will behave accordingly.

Thoughts: "I'm going to be late for work. My boss will be mad at me."

Feelings: Anxious, nervous, agitated.

Actions: Driving fast/aggressively, taking risks, changing your route.

The relationship between thoughts, feelings, and behaviors is addressed in the SSET program, which presents and encourages the practice of skills that shift the way that youth think, feel, and behave in situations to make their experiences of the situations better, if possible.

We address each of the three components in different ways, as shown in Table 2.

Table 2—How SSET Addresses the Three Components

Component	SSET Teaching
Thoughts	• Teach students to notice their thinking. • Teach students to challenge their thinking, or to challenge their harmful thoughts to have more balanced and accurate thoughts. • Teach students to stop negative or problematic thoughts that are getting in their way.
Feelings	• Teach students to relax their bodies. • Help reduce the anxiety related to the trauma that happened to them. • Help reduce the anxiety students feel when they are reminded of what happened to them.
Behaviors	• Teach students to consider alternatives for what to do when there is a problem. • Teach students to decide on a plan of action and carry out their desired plan.

Why Do We Address Thoughts in Trauma Survivors?

Research shows that thinking is disturbed after an extreme trauma or experience with violence. Two general themes begin to push away normal thoughts:

The world is dangerous. I am not safe. People cannot be trusted.

I can't deal with this. I'll never be the same. I am falling apart.

These two ideas or "themes" in thinking can really interfere with daily life. In the SSET program, we look for times when these themes are getting in the way and then teach students to "challenge" them to make sure their thoughts are accurate and balanced. Usually, students can find a more adaptive, less distressing way of looking at the problems they are facing.

How Do We Reduce Anxiety Related to the Trauma or to Reminders of the Trauma?

The SSET program reduces anxiety related to the traumatic experience by capitalizing on the human process called **habituation**. The human body cannot stay highly aroused for long periods of time—the natural process is for anxiety to gradually decline.

Imagine climbing to the top of a very tall tower. Most of us would feel some anxiety or fear at first. But as you stay up there (and nothing bad happens), gradually that fear or anxiety will decrease. If you stay up there for a few days, it will become a second home. This demonstrates the way that the body adjusts to situations that start out frightening (as long as nothing bad happens to re-arouse the fear).

In the SSET group, we work toward students "getting used to" writing, thinking, or talking about their trauma in the safety of the support group. Thus, their anxiety gradually decreases. As an added bonus, the writing and sharing can also enable students to process or digest their experience. That is, the more they are able to process the experience—first in a factual, less threatening form, and later by adding details and associated emotions—the easier it will become to continue doing so and the less these thoughts and the anxiety they cause will interfere with their functioning. The goals are for students (1) to feel that although a terrible thing happened to them, it cannot hurt them now and (2) to understand that thinking, talking, or writing about what happened is not dangerous and gets easier the more they are able to do it.

SSET does the same thing for reminders of the trauma, such as situations involving people, places, or things that make the student feel anxious or upset because they are reminders of what happened. In the SSET program, students identify the situations they are avoiding and set about deliberately confronting them instead of avoiding them. As students are gradually able to approach and endure these situations without anything bad happening, they gain a sense of mastery over the situation, and their associated anxiety decreases.

Selecting Students for SSET

SSET is intended for middle school students who have experienced a significant trauma and who are experiencing considerable distress related to that event. We recommend using a screening instrument among as many students as possible in the student body in order to identify students in need of this program. We usually use a version that includes

- a scale assessing exposure to community violence (but not violence at home) and other traumatic events
- a scale assessing anxiety and nervousness related to that exposure.

There are many different scales that would be appropriate for this process, and each has its own guideline for scoring.[3]

Because students' responses on self-report measures are not always valid, it is important to follow up the screening process with a personal interview in which you review and confirm the responses with the student and make sure that the student is interested in participating in and appropriate for the SSET program. Please refer to the instructions provided in "Forming and Scheduling Groups" (pp. 19–23).

In inner-city schools, it is expected that many students (upwards of 20 percent) would benefit from this kind of intervention. In other areas, the proportion of students who would benefit may be smaller. If an entire school has been affected by a disaster or violence, it is possible that many more than 20 percent of students would benefit from this kind of intervention. In these cases, school counselors should wait three to six months after the trauma before identifying those in need.

Who Gives Permission for Screening?

Parents give permission for screening prior to it taking place, and they are told about the purpose (i.e., identifying students who might benefit from the SSET program).

We provide a sample letter in Figure 2 on the next page, but you should follow your school's procedures that establish the types of letters and permissions required.

---

[3] The measures we used in our pilot study for SSET are available upon request from Lisa Jaycox (jaycox@rand.org).

Figure 2—Sample Letter and Permission Form for Parents

Date: _____

Dear Parents,

[*School name*] is fortunate to have a special counseling program for students who have experienced stressful events. We have found that students who have experienced trauma as victims or witnesses often suffer from a unique kind of stress called *traumatic stress*. It could show up in the form of your child not wanting to go to school or as difficulties with schoolwork and concentration.

We would like your permission to ask your child some questions about whether he or she has experienced or witnessed stressful events. Examples of questions that we will ask your child are "Have you been in a serious accident where you could have been badly hurt or could have been killed?" and "Has anyone very close to you been very sick or injured?" In addition, we will ask your child whether he or she has been experiencing trouble with falling and staying asleep or is experiencing bad dreams or nightmares due to the experience. These questions will help us determine if the academic and/or social problems your child may be having are due to one or more stressful events that he or she might have experienced or witnessed.

All of the information collected will be used to try to improve your child's emotional well-being, his or her academic success, and the overall success of the school. If we find that your child has been a victim or witness to a stressful event, we hope to be able to offer a support group that will help him or her deal with any problems in a constructive way that we hope will improve his or her grades and attendance. The information that we collect will be kept confidential and will not be a part of your child's school record.

If you would like your child to participate and wish to give us permission to ask your child questions related to stressful events, please sign the bottom of this form. If you have any questions related to this program or would like to review a copy of the questions that we will be asking your child, please contact me at [*contact info*].

Thank you for your cooperation and support.

Sincerely,

— —

Student name: _____   Student date of birth: _____

❑ I accept

❑ I do not accept

Parent signature: _____   Date: _____

Is SSET Appropriate for Everyone Who Screens In?

No, not necessarily. SSET is designed as a support group, but some students will need more-intensive, personalized professional help. A student with a high score on the screening measures may be included in the group, but may need extra help in addition to the groups. Students with other signs of risk (e.g., engaging in risky behaviors, severely depressed, missing school, disclosing child abuse or a desire to hurt themselves or others) should be immediately linked with a clinician. Depending on the circumstances, such students could still be included in the groups if other, more-intensive services are also in place. Discuss such students as a team with a clinician and the parents to decide what is right for the student.

Where Does Screening Occur?

Screening can occur in groups of students if they can be seated far enough apart to keep their answers private. We generally read the screening questions aloud, and the students follow along and mark their answers.

How Are Parents Notified of Positive Screens, and What Should They Be Told?

When students screen positive (i.e., they report significant exposure to violence and problems related to trauma), parents are notified by telephone whenever possible. Parents are informed that, based on the results of the screening, their child is eligible for and may benefit from the SSET program. In other words, their child reported being exposed to some type of stressful or violent event and is worried about it. We remind parents that their child's answers are confidential (as they were informed at the consent phase), but that most children (usually 80 percent) report seeing fights or verbal threats in their communities. We emphasize that the group is intended to (1) help children manage their feelings about these stressful events so that they can cope with them better and (2) improve their communication with their parents about their feelings. We invite parents to ask questions about the program. If parents are interested, they complete an informed-consent process at that time. We then share details of the group meeting schedule and our expectations for participation in and completion of the groups.

What About Parents of Students Who Screen Negative?

Parents are informed at the consent phase that if their child qualifies for the program, they will be contacted. The parents of students who do not screen positive are not contacted.

Forming and Scheduling Groups

What Kind of Space Is Needed for the Groups?

Identify where the groups can take place and ensure that the space is available for the entire 10-week period. The space should include a table and be large enough to accommodate 8–10 people. A dry-erase board or easel is needed for group activities. The space should also be private so that others cannot hear the discussions. If possible, select a room with a large table that students can sit around; this helps make students feel comfortable and differentiates the setting a bit from a traditional classroom.

Is There an Optimal Time of Day for the Intervention?

Each school may have a preference for when the groups are held. Some schools request the groups be held after school hours, while some prefer holding the groups during school. If groups are held during the school day, establish if there is a preference for when students attend the meetings, such as during nonacademic courses or free time.

Is There an Optimal Time of Year for Intervention?

Review the school calendar with administrators to identify important events, such as standardized testing, holidays, and school activities. Ten continuous weeks is optimal but not always realistic. Identify the time of year to implement the program that will be the least disruptive. If you cannot identify a block of ten weeks for the program, you can hold two lessons in some weeks to shorten the overall length of the program. The ideal lessons for doubling up are Lessons Two through Five or Lessons Eight through Ten. Keep Lessons Six and Seven in separate weeks, if possible.

Who Has Permission to Participate in the Group?

The parents whose children screen positive for the group are contacted initially by telephone. Usually, they must provide written consent for the child to participate in the group.

How Are the Groups Formed?

Once students have been identified for the group, it is important to meet individually with them to verify their appropriateness for the group. Students can be excused from class for these appointments if the school agrees; otherwise, the appointment should be scheduled during lunch or recess. The individual interview allows the leader to review the symptoms that the students have endorsed; assist students in identifying the traumatic event that is currently the most distressing/interfering and that they want to work on in the group, ensuring that the choice is appropriate for group work; and describe the group to the students to assess their interest in participation. Questions and areas of discussion are presented below:

- Using the screener, review the exposure to violence reported by the student. Ask questions about what the student meant when he or she endorsed significant or life-threatening violence. If there are several traumas, try to ascertain which one or more are most difficult or bothersome at the present time.
- Using the screener, review problems endorsed.
  - If the trauma endorsed was significant
    - o and if the student continues to endorse symptoms, describe the group and explain that the student will be asked in the support group to write and talk about the identified trauma(s).
    - o and if the student no longer endorses symptoms, consider excluding the student from the group.
- If no significant trauma was endorsed
  - and if the student continues to endorse symptoms, refer to clinical backup for consultation.
  - and if the student no longer endorses symptoms, consider excluding the student from the group.
- Discuss all possible exclusions with the supervisor or a clinical consultant.
- Be prepared to handle disclosures of child abuse that come up in this meeting. Be aware of school procedures for handling such disclosures, and have the clinician backup information handy so that you can consult with the clinician as necessary. (See "Clinical Backup and Consultation," pp. 33–35.)

How Many Kids Are in One Group?

The typical number is six to ten students per group, with one or two facilitators. If you are forming more than one group at a time, you can look through the list of students and think about what groupings would maximize participation and minimize disruption, based on the students' normal behavior and relationships in school.

Do You Segregate the Groups, or Have Boys and Girls Together?

Most groups have been conducted with both boys and girls together, provided that there are at least two members of each gender in the group. A sole boy or girl might feel uncomfortable alone in the group.

Do You Have Bullies and Victims in the Same Group? What About Kids Suffering from Different Kinds of Trauma?

Bullies and victims can be in the same group together; in our experience, this has not been an issue. In special circumstances, it may be necessary to separate them if you feel the combination will interfere with the dynamic of the group. There are typically a range of traumatic events disclosed in the group, so one student's trauma does not usually stand apart from the others. Identifying each student's trauma prior to the first group is helpful for planning, but is not necessarily a factor in forming the groups.

What If There Are Racial Tensions in the School?

Sometimes issues can arise if there are racial or ethnic tensions in the school and the group includes a mixture of races or ethnic groups. As with mixing gender and bullies/victims in the same group, careful formation of groups may be required to make sure that there are adequate numbers of members of each group and that the group will feel safe for all members.

Some guidelines for respecting all group members include the following:

- Recognize that students and group leaders sometimes hold negative attitudes about people who are different from themselves.
- Strive to understand and gain knowledge about the different ethnic groups in your group by asking questions, listening carefully, and encouraging students in the group to do the same.
- Use diversity as a topic to help convey group concepts. For instance, the Helpful Thinking questions taught in Lesson Four can be used to challenge common assumptions and stereotypes about different racial or ethnic groups. The diversity of the group members may help to dispel some of these unhelpful ways of thinking.

- Be flexible in your approach to students and parents of students who come from a different culture than yours, being sure to respect cultural and familial beliefs and practices that may differ from your own.
- Ask for input from group members on how to make the group a better and safer place for them.

What If a Student Misses a Lesson or Multiple Lessons?

Depending on the circumstance, you may want to meet with the student individually to catch him or her up on the missed lesson. This is especially important if he or she misses the first group meeting, which establishes the groundwork for the remaining groups and addresses confidentiality. If a student misses a later lesson and it is not possible to meet with him or her individually, he or she can usually catch up with the group during the homework review that takes places at the beginning of group. It is also helpful to have group members review for each other the previous lesson content.

If a student misses multiple lessons, it may make sense to remove him or her from the group, but this can be discussed with the student to determine his or her preferences. You can also discuss it with the group in terms of whether they will feel comfortable with the student rejoining the group or discussing what they can do to make themselves more comfortable. If another group will run later in the school year, students who missed multiple lessons could perhaps join that group instead.

How Do Students Get to and from Groups?

If the groups are held during school hours, strategize with administrators regarding how to get students to and from the group. For example, if students need to be escorted in the halls, identify who has permission and availability to do that, keeping in mind confidentiality. If the group is held at the same time each day, perhaps students can come directly to the group and then return to class with a permission slip. Permission slips or passes can be prepared ahead of time and given to the teachers as a reminder to release the students. Having runners or school staff available to help can be very useful. This important logistical piece can affect the organization of the groups, including the length of time needed for each meeting.

How Should the Groups Be Scheduled?

Depending on school preferences, groups may be held each week at the same day and time or at various times to avoid having students miss too much of one class. Discuss scheduling issues with the administrators and prepare to be flexible. To avoid conflicts with academic classes, consider choosing a time when students are in electives. If that is not possible, rotating the meeting time each week will cause each student to miss a particular class just one or two times instead of every week. After-school time slots may seem like a good solution, but our experience is that attendance suffers greatly if group is held after school. Table 3 presents a sample meeting schedule. Note that due to missing a week for spring break, Lessons Eight and Nine are held during the same week.

Table 3—Sample Meeting Schedule

Date	Lesson	Lesson Title (Leader Activity)
March 14	One	Introduction (contact parents)
March 21	Two	Common Reactions to Trauma and Strategies for Relaxation
March 28	N/A	No group—school district spring break
April 4	Three	Thoughts and Feelings
April 11	Four	Helpful Thinking (contact parents)
April 18	Five	Facing Your Fears
April 25	Six	Trauma Narrative, Part One
May 2	Seven	Trauma Narrative, Part Two
May 9 & May 12	Eight & Nine	Problem Solving
May 16	Ten	Planning for the Future and Graduation (contact parents)

What About Teacher Support?

Teacher support is particularly important if the groups take place during the school day and cause students to miss class. The first strategy for gaining teacher support is to speak to teachers in advance of the group in a prearranged meeting that provides information about the program, including the need, the purpose, and the predicted outcomes. Invite questions and input to help teachers feel they are part of the process. Once students are identified for the groups, send teachers a letter informing them which students will be pulled from class. At the group's conclusion, another meeting can be held to provide teachers with feedback and information about the (general) results of the program to help them see the positive gains. Remember, though, that no personal student information can be shared outside the group. Group leaders need to refrain from making comments about students to other school staff and students in order to protect the confidentiality of the SSET group.

Dealing with Trauma and Violence Exposure

Traumatized Students

Working with stress or trauma survivors requires sensitivity and patience. There are several points that are important to keep in mind:

- Students who have been exposed to violence and who are symptomatic may be guarded and slow to trust. Careful explanation of group procedures and rationales for all the components of the program can help to build trust and gain compliance. Make sure that all group members understand the concept of confidentiality, and try to build a cohesive group that feels safe to all group members.
- Such students may overreact to real or perceived injustices, so group leaders need to be consistent and predictable.
- Students often tend to "reenact" the stress or trauma and can sometimes try to provoke adults into being abusive. Don't fall into this trap. Check your own anger and frustration often, and make sure that you do not in any way feed into the cycle of abuse that the students are accustomed to.
- Students who have been traumatized get scared easily. Be conservative in the use of physical contact, and always ask permission before unexpectedly touching a group member (unless it is a matter of safety).

As the group leader, you will benefit from remembering that **these students are resilient and have developed creative ways to cope with devastating events**. This will help you stay compassionate and empathic when they act up!

Common Group Leader Concerns

Table 4 on the next page presents some common misconceptions about processing trauma experiences that it is important to address.

Table 4—Common Misconceptions About Processing Trauma

Common Concern	Actual Experience of SSET Leaders
If I ask a student to write or share what happened to him or her, I will be retraumatizing him or her.	Students are generally relieved to have the chance to talk about their traumatic experience. They often have found it difficult to talk to others, and they sometimes believe that no one else wants to hear about what happened to them. It gives them a controlled, supportive environment for expressing their feelings.
I'm not sure I can take hearing about all these traumas myself.	It is true that it can be hard for group leaders to hear the stories of their students. Group leaders can find it rather intense and can have their own intrusive thoughts, nightmares, and the like, but these reactions do not typically last very long. The reward of helping students move through these experiences usually outweighs the "compassion fatigue" that group leaders can experience. Supervision and consultation with peers can help alleviate this distress. (See "Clinical Backup and Consultation," pp. 33–35.)
The students will fall apart when they try to share their trauma.	In our experience to date, this has not happened. Students show remarkable resilience and are able to do these exercises quite well. As mentioned above, they are usually eager to talk to people who will listen to them about what happened.

Working with Students Who Have Been Multiply Traumatized or Abused

The SSET program is built to help address a specific trauma or violent experience in each student's life. However, it is typical for students to have experienced several traumatic events of different types at various points in their lives. For example, students often had prior experiences with

- being bullied
- car accidents or sudden injuries
- the sudden death of a family member or friend
- a serious, life-threatening illness
- being abused by a trusted caregiver (see discussion below)
- witnessing domestic violence at home.

Therefore, group leaders often have to help students "choose" what they will focus on in the group lessons. The key question to ask is,

Which event is most upsetting at present?

It is normally best to focus during the group on the most upsetting traumatic event (particularly in Lessons Six and Seven, when students write and share their traumatic experience). As distress related to that event begins to subside, you can turn to less troublesome events. You may find it possible to work on several events with some students and on just one event with others. It is important that the child make this decision, as the trauma that is currently most troublesome for the student is not necessarily the one that an outsider would judge as the most severe.

What If the Student Has Been Abused by a Trusted Caregiver?

- We recommend that students do not focus on their child-abuse experiences (particularly sexual abuse) in the group, but focus instead on one of the other events they have experienced.
- You will need to follow your school's procedures for reporting or handling child abuse.

- You will need to refer these children into counseling to deal with the child abuse, and you will need to consult with a clinician about whether the group might still be helpful for these students.
- You will have to make a report to authorities in all cases of suspected child abuse, following normal procedures at your school.

Disclosure by Group Members

Some Students Do Not Share as Much as You Think They Should

When students are hesitant to share information about themselves and their experiences, it is important to provide some of the following types of support and encouragement:

- Validate that it can be difficult to talk about an experience with violence or trauma, especially when doing so is new.
- Remind students that beginning to share their experiences is the purpose of the group and one of the main ways that they will start to help themselves feel better.
- Break down the disclosure into a smaller piece. For example, ask students to share any small part of their experience or write something down to then read (or have you read on their behalf).
- Try to engage hesitant students in less-threatening ways in the group, such as asking them to offer examples or answer questions regarding other nonpersonal group content. Any positive experience with participating in the group in any way will build students' sense of comfort and confidence, leading to a better chance of self-disclosure when the time is appropriate.
- Meet briefly with very hesitant students outside of group to strategize a plan for making disclosure easier. For example, some students may prefer to share first and "get it over with" so they can relax for the remainder of the group, while others may prefer to go last or in the middle after others have already shared. Disclosure may be made easier or more difficult for students by where they are sitting and who is sitting next to or across from them. Helping to orchestrate these types of logistical factors may help to decrease students' anxiety and therefore increase the chances that they will feel comfortable enough to disclose in the group.

Other Students Share More Than You Think They Should

When students tend to be overly talkative and disclose more information than may be appropriate for the group, it will be important to employ some of the following strategies to redirect them:

- Interrupt with a positive statement, such as "Thank you for sharing that" or "Okay, that gives us a good idea of your experience."
- Remind students that the group is for everyone, and that all must share the responsibility of leaving time for everyone to participate.
- Set a time to talk more later. Remind students that there will be other groups for them to continue sharing, and suggest returning to the problem at a later time.
- Meet with them individually outside of the group to make a concrete plan for what they will share in a particular group. Reviewing and providing an explanation for the boundaries will likely be useful.

Disclosure by Group Leaders

It is essential to remember that the group exists to serve the purpose of supporting students with trauma experiences. The focus of the groups should always be on the students' experiences (and not those of the leader).

Given that SSET leaders are working and sometimes living in the same communities where these students experienced traumatic events, it is likely that group leaders will also have some of their own trauma experiences with the same or entirely different events. But it is usually not that advantageous for group members to hear about their group leaders' personal experiences. To think this through, you can ask yourself the following questions:

- Is sharing this information going to be helpful to the group?
- Is sharing this information going to be helpful to me?
- Will I regret sharing this information later?
- Why do I feel the need to talk about this?

The general rule is **if in doubt, do NOT share**.

That said, there may be some appropriate times for limited self-disclosure in the group, especially for demonstrative purposes. For example, it would be appropriate when discussing Hot Seat thoughts in Lessons Three and Four for teachers to talk about how automatic thoughts and helpful thoughts affected them during their first day of teaching a class or during their first teacher-parent meetings. For example, a teacher might say

> *"The very first day I got up in front of a class, I was thinking, 'Oh no, what if I trip, what if I forget what I'm saying and they laugh at me.' But I used Hot Seat thoughts to help me out by telling myself, 'It's not likely that I'll trip, I don't hear of that happening much, and even if I did trip, I could make a joke out of it to get the class laughing with me; and even if I do say something different, the class won't notice because they don't know what I planned to say anyway; I'm pretty good at this kind of thing, I don't have to be perfect, but I've done well in the past.'"*

However, it would **not** be appropriate to disclose automatic and helpful thoughts used to deal with conflict involving a parent, student, coworker, employer, or teacher's union.

As another example, it may be appropriate to use self-disclosure about how you problem-solved when you forgot your teaching materials for a lesson one day. For example, you

- came up with several options: start crying, do a different lesson that day, ask another teacher to borrow hers, go home at lunch to get them

- evaluated the pros and cons of each option
- chose one option
- evaluated the outcome.

It would not be appropriate, however, to discuss how you problem-solved a disagreement with your significant other, your own children, or a neighbor. **Your personal life should be "off-limits" for discussion in the group.**

Clinical Backup and Consultation

A decision to run the SSET support program should begin with deciding whether there is adequate clinical backup available within the school or school district. Beginning with screening students for the group, there will be times during the course of the SSET groups that you need clinical backup support or have questions about the concepts you are delivering in group. Each group leader should have a designated clinician for SSET—a school counselor, consultant, or school-district social worker—who can be on call for you while you are running the groups. The clinician should be available to assist with any concerns leaders have regarding the well-being of a student involved in the SSET groups.

If you are concerned about a student's well-being or any aspect of his or her care or participation in the group, you should call your clinical backup to discuss the student and to ascertain whether further services or intervention may be necessary.

When deciding which students to include in the groups, include the clinician and review scores and screeners along with any other information available about the candidates. Some students will need more-intensive professional help in addition to, or instead of, SSET.

The following issues **require immediate (i.e., within 24 hours) discussion with a clinician**; you should also follow existing procedures at your school on the same school day. If you encounter any of the following situations, you should call the clinician to alert him or her that you need to discuss the situation immediately. These situations include

- suspected or disclosed child abuse (e.g., physical or sexual abuse, witnessing domestic violence, or neglect)
- concern that a student has a plan to harm another student
- disclosure of a student's wish or plan to harm or try to kill himself or herself
- a student whose emotional state seems like more than you can handle, or whose emotional state is worsening.

These things may not necessarily exclude a student from group participation, but a clinical backup will need to be aware of these issues to help decide (1) whether the group is appropriate for the student, (2) whether there are any other services that may be necessary and in the best clinical interest of the student, and (3) whether there are any mandatory reporting obligations that you are responsible for.

For other situations, we strongly **recommend clinical consultation prior to the subsequent group.** You can discuss these situations in your weekly supervision meeting. Such situations include

- family issues that emerge (such as a parent's substance abuse problem)
- concern that your own issues (such as a fear about recurring violence) are interfering with the group process
- a need for assistance with ideas about how to manage group dynamics
- student behavioral issues.

Clinicians should also be included at the end of groups to ensure that any group member who needs continued support will receive it.

Essentially, if at any point a leader feels that he or she is not adequately trained to address or manage any issues related to the individual students' or group's well-being, then clinical consultation should be sought. Figure 3 on the next page presents a model SSET referral form that you could use to seek a consult for a student in your group.

Consultation on the content of the SSET program should be sought when there are questions regarding the concepts to be delivered in the group (e.g., education, relaxation, helpful thoughts, trauma narrative, facing fears, problem solving) or the best way to present salient examples of such concepts. Consultation with the SSET trainer may also be helpful if a leader is grappling with the theory or reasons behind some of the concepts.

Self-Care Is Also Important

Working with traumatized students is an intense and sometimes difficult experience. The following are signs that the work is interfering with your life too much:

- You are dreaming about the traumas that happened to your students, or thoughts about their traumatic events are popping into your own head.
- You are having trouble sleeping or concentrating, or you are feeling irritable and angry more than is usual.
- You are feeling more vulnerable than usual, or you are jumpy and easily startled.
- The opposite of the above, in that you feel numb to what the students are telling you and you feel unable to feel the range of emotions you usually feel.

These are signs of "compassion fatigue" or "burnout." They are a normal reaction to working with trauma. The remedy is to talk to colleagues or friends, or to consult with the clinician for the project or with the SSET experts in order to regain a sense of balance in your life.

Figure 3—SSET Referral Form

Student name: _____   Student ID number: _____

School: _____   Grade: _____

    This student is participating in a Support for Students Exposed to Trauma (SSET) group that I am running. We are currently on lesson ____ of ten lessons, and the group is planned to end on _____.

    I am referring this student to you for the following reason(s):

_____

_____

_____

_____

_____

    I consider this request to be:

    ❑ urgent (I have called you and left a message as well)

    ❑ routine

    I would appreciate a follow-up call to tell me that you received this form and to inform me of any action steps your are taking.

Thank you,

SSET Leader: _____   Date: _____

Special Student and Group Issues

There may be times when a student's level or spirit of participation or reactions in group do not meet your expectations and may impact the group as a whole. Some guidance follows for managing these issues if they arise.

A Student Exhibits Bravado or Minimizes the Problem

A variety of factors (e.g., comfort level with discussing personal information, issues of trust, accustomed role in a social group) may influence a student's responses and reactions in group. Although it can be disconcerting when a student puts on a brave façade or front, as if what happened or what is being discussed is "no big deal," it is important that the leader remembers that these reactions are ways of adapting to trauma and violence and that the student may in fact still be benefiting from the group.

In this situation it may be helpful to **talk about how *others* may feel in the situation** to make the student more comfortable with verbalizing his or her own negative feelings. For example,

> *"Okay, so you feel like it's no big thing for you, and I want to thank you for sharing your feelings about that with us. Because we all react differently to different situations I think that many of us would agree that being threatened in the schoolyard could be a really frightening thing."*

In addition, it may be helpful to refer back to some of the problems that this student has acknowledged in the past related to the event. For example,

> *"Sometimes even though we think something isn't such a big deal, we still find ourselves thinking about it later, feeling on edge or angry, and avoiding those people or the place it happened and even other things that we didn't used to avoid."*

It is important that these interactions adopt an accepting and generalizing tone and not one that is argumentative. It is not necessary to "call out" the student or get him or her to admit deeper feelings. If a student continues to deny that is the case for him or her, it may be best to deflect the attention from him or her and move on, allowing the student to save face.

A Student Is Wrong

If a student answers a question incorrectly, it is important to

- acknowledge him or her for participating
- restate whatever points the student has made that may apply to other group content
- re-ask the question to give the student a chance to answer correctly.

If the student still cannot answer, open up the question to the rest of the group. Several examples follow.

Example 1

- Leader: *"What's the first step in solving this problem?"*
- Student: *"Telling a teacher."*
- Leader: *"Okay, good. You just gave us a good idea for one option for how to respond. Can you tell me what we may want to create before we ever make the decision about which way to respond?"*

Example 2

- Leader: *"Can anyone think of an automatic or unhelpful thought that someone may have in this situation?"*
- Student: *"They may not even be talking about me."*
- Leader: *"Okay. You just gave us a great example of a Hot Seat thought. That thought may actually be helpful if it's realistic. Now can you think of a more unhelpful thought that may jump into someone's mind in this situation and get them feeling bad?"*

Example 3

- Leader: *"Who remembers what we talked about last week?"*
- Student: *"Relaxation and breathing right."*
- Leader: *"Thanks. That is something we talked about a few weeks ago, and you are right, I think last week we might have mentioned how relaxation can be useful throughout the group and even afterward. Can you remember what the new focus of group was last week that you were all asked to practice this week?"*

A Student Is Gossiping Outside of Group (i.e., Breaking Confidentiality)

Confidentiality is critical to any group and to the comfort of its participating members. At the beginning of the group, students typically pick up on the seriousness of this from the group leader and each other and take the signing of the confidentiality agreement very seriously. In our experience, there have been very few incidents of students actually breaking confidentiality. That being said, a breach of confidentiality, which occurs when a student discloses *outside* the group something said *inside* the group by anyone other than himself or herself, is very serious, and the consequences should reflect that.

Typically, it is appropriate to meet separately with the parties involved to discuss what occurred and determine whether a breach actually occurred. If there has been a breach, the offending student should be removed from the group pending implementation of a consequence or some form of compensation. For example, the student could be told that he or she will not be allowed to return to group without a verbal or written apology to the member harmed by the breach and a promise to all group members that such a breach will not happen again. Another way of handling it would be to have the group (with the offending student not present) vote about whether it feels comfortable allowing the student to return. If a student does lose the privilege of being in group, it is important to speak with clinical backup about getting alternative care for him or her.

Students Are Gossiping Inside of Group (i.e., Talking About Non-Group People)

When gossip occurs in the group, whether about other students, teachers, or the school administration, it is important to curb it early on. That is, make it clear that the group is a place for students to share their own ideas and stories so that they can feel and function better, and that those are the stories you are interested in. It is not the place to share information about people not involved in the group. It may be appropriate to make a statement about how others may be hurt by a discussion of this information behind their backs; you could even consider referring the students to some of the thoughts and feelings information they have gleaned from group. Clearly, there may be times when students or school staff outside the group are an integral part of a student's story or example. You may want to make a group rule about not using names of people outside of group, or ask students to use first names only or introduce only relevant information into discussion so that group does not become a gossip session about, for example, a particular bully, bus driver, teacher, or neighbor.

A Student Is Unsupportive of Others

Students may have a hard time being supportive in the group setting for a variety of reasons. Some students may simply lack the skills to know how to act in a supportive way. Thus, it may be useful to provide concrete examples to the group about ways they may show support for one another. For example,

- making eye contact when listening
- not talking while someone else is speaking
- making supportive statements (e.g., "That sounds scary," "That must have been hard," "I know what you mean")

- making positive statements (e.g., "That was a good example/idea," "I liked the way you did your drawing")
- sitting still
- making supportive looks or gestures.

If a student is being unsupportive in group, it is appropriate to meet with him or her individually to (1) review some of these skills for showing support and (2) further assess the situation (e.g., is he or she being unsupportive of everyone, or just one member?). Once you have an idea about what may be going on, it will be helpful to implement a plan. For example, if a student is generally unsupportive but not necessarily disrespectful in the group, providing the student with both an individual reminder of supportive behaviors that you would like to see him or her using in group and some coaching around these behaviors may eliminate the problem. If, on the other hand, a student is unsupportive in a disrespectful way despite your reminders in an individual meeting, then he or she may need to be removed from the group and referred for other treatment. If there is an issue between two students, it may help to seek advice from your clinical backup as to how to assist them in resolving the issue at least for the purposes of respecting and supporting one another in the group.

A Student Is Unmotivated

When a student appears to be unmotivated to participate in group, in the independent practice, or both, it can sometimes be helpful to remind the student of what he or she said he or she wanted to get out of the group. A general reminder that all of the different skills that are included in group are aimed at helping the student achieve the goals of feeling and functioning better—goals identified in the first group—can be useful. It may also be helpful to provide a skill-building analogy for all the practice he or she is being asked to do and linking that practice to the goal. For example,

"I know that many of you wanted to feel happier and less nervous and be able to do all of the fun activities that you used to do or get along better with your family. All of the things that we are learning about and practicing in group can directly help you with those things. I want you to be able to feel better and do everything you want to do, and that's why we have these groups.

"I can't do the practice for you, though. You know how in basketball you have to do a lot of drills at practice that would look really silly if you did them during an actual game, but they actually help your performance in the game? And you know how when you learn the piano you practice lots of scales that you would never do in your recital, but they help your performance at the recital?

"Well, our groups are kind of like that. There are a lot of practice drills about changing the way we think about things, thinking through options for making a situation easier for us to handle, and learning to relax our bodies even when we aren't feeling nervous or on edge. Well, all of this practice will help you feel better and be able to do what you want to do in the real game—which is your life."

For some students, lack of motivation may come from feeling overwhelmed. For these students, it may be useful to spend some time breaking concepts or practice down into smaller pieces and troubleshooting obstacles for completing independent practice, group participation, or both.

A Student Is Disruptive

Students may be disruptive in group for a variety of reasons, including

- difficulty focusing attention and sitting still
- lack of cognitive ability
- discomfort with the material.

Whatever the cause, it may be useful to set up a "program" to increase the student's motivation and help him or her keep on track. For example,

- If a student is constantly speaking out in a disruptive way, you could assign him or her three or four index cards that can be used during each group. Ask the student to give you a card each time that he or she takes the floor during group. Once all of the cards are used, he or she must wait until the next group to share.
- If a student disrupts group by making jokes or clowning around, you could give the student a point every time there is a 10-minute period that there is no clowning behavior. If he or she earns four points in any one lesson, he or she may get a small reward (e.g., a toy, trinket, or treat).
- If a student is impulsive and unaware of his or her disruptive behaviors, it can be useful to meet individually to come up with a signal that you give when you notice it. You could create a rule that the student is allowed four signals per group before a consequence, such as leaving for the remainder of the group, is implemented.

Typically, disruptive behavior can be managed with some thought given to a plan for the individual student. In addition, student behavior improves with time in the group as trust, comfort, and cohesiveness also further develop.

A Student Is Seriously Disruptive

If a student is seriously disruptive during the lessons, he or she is likely to undermine the group for all the participants. Thus, it is important to either get the student to act more appropriately or to remove the student from the group. If the disruption is violent or if the student is breaking group confidentiality, these are grounds for removing the student from the group immediately. You will also need to explain to the rest of the group what happened, and you can use some of the skills taught in the lessons to help the group members deal with the change. For instance, if the student was violent, you can ask the students in the group to identify the thoughts, feelings, and behaviors they experienced at the time that that happened.

Students Create a Consistently Negative or Unhelpful Group Atmosphere

It is important to make sure that students participate in the group in a constructive manner. Some program developers and researchers have found that students can learn negative behaviors from one another in groups, a pattern known as "deviancy training." Usually, students will regulate the group themselves and make it a constructive atmosphere, but if they do not, then the group leader must step in. This may involve removing members of the group who, rather than focusing on the constructive, skill-building emphasis of the group, instead provide negative or maladaptive suggestions to others.

Matching Problems and Goals

Although the SSET program is designed for groups of students, it is most effective when the group leader thinks about each student's problems and the corresponding goals in the group (see Table 5). The "Problems/Goals Worksheet" found in Figure 4 on the next page facilitates the conceptualization of needs for each participant. We recommend that group leaders complete this worksheet for each participant prior to the second or third group meeting. Review and modify the individual worksheets during supervision and periodically throughout treatment.

Table 5—Primary Problems and Support Group Goals

Primary Problems	Emphasis in Support Group
Severe general anxiety	Relaxation, alternative coping strategies
Nightmares, flashbacks, intrusive thinking	Writing and sharing the trauma narrative
Severe situational anxiety	Facing your fears, helpful thinking
Avoidance of stress or trauma reminders	Facing your fears
Guilt	Helpful thinking
Shame	Writing and sharing the trauma narrative
Grief/sadness/loss	Writing and sharing the trauma narrative
Poor self-concept	Facing your fears, helpful thinking
Problems with peers or family	Problem solving
Impulsivity	Problem solving

Figure 4—Matching Problems and Goals Worksheet

School:	Student Name:
Group:	Group Leader:
Student's Stated Goals:	Parent's Stated Goals:
Primary Problems: *(List the student's problems that you know about.)*	Emphasis in Support Group: *(List the group elements that might help with each problem.)*
Special Issues: *(List any family, school, or social issues that you need to remember during groups with this student.)*	
Progress in Group/Changes in Plan: *(List any issues that arise or changes that occur during the support groups, e.g., change in focus from one traumatic event to another.)*	

Homework Assignments

Unlike most academic homework, independent practice for the group involves asking students to do things that may make them feel very uncomfortable. Although this is part of what helps students eventually feel better, it is important to acknowledge how difficult it may be and to know that homework compliance is typically low for a variety of reasons:

- the discomfort of facing fears
- a lack of time (due to academic homework, after school-activities, sibling-care responsibilities, etc.)
- not understanding homework instructions
- logistical issues, such as transportation.

While it is important to troubleshoot obstacles to homework completion and try to motivate students to follow through on the assignments, it is equally important that **lack of homework compliance not be viewed or treated as a failure.** Independent practice for SSET is not like homework from academic classrooms, and **youth should never be made to feel that they are being marked down, given a poor grade, or thought of in a negative light by group leaders or group members because of lack of completion. In fact, it is not abnormal to have less than half of independent practices completed!**

However, a couple of things may help encourage students to complete assignments:

- Some students may respond to reinforcement for homework completed. In general, it will be important to offer direct verbal and public praise for any homework compliance (e.g., "Great job," high five, pat on the shoulder, stickers, smiles). Consider acknowledging even partially completed homework and homework that a student relates verbally even if she or he forgot the paperwork.
- You may also want to offer a more concrete reward system. For example, a point chart could display points students earn for each assignment completed. Points could lead to participation in a final activity (e.g., a pizza party) or be traded for a gift certificate, small toy, food, or other prize. Ensure that the point system is set up to allow all group members to claim some reward.
- Reinforcement could also be given on a daily basis during each homework review. It may work to offer two points (or two donuts or two Koosh balls, etc.) to those who bring their completed independent practice to group, and to offer one point (or small prize) to those who are able to complete the assignment in the group during the homework review.
- Enable students to complete the practice during the homework review. For example, if a student did not fill out his or her Hot Seat worksheet prior to the lesson, he or she may

still be able to think of a situation that occurred since the last group and fill out the worksheet or work through it verbally in the group.

- Enable students to begin their homework at the end of the lesson after you describe the assignment. It is especially helpful to start it off by writing in a problem or situation so that they know exactly what to work on.

Privacy of the Homework Forms

Since the homework forms cover private issues, it is important to talk to students about **where they will keep them and how they will protect their own privacy.** Some students may not feel comfortable taking assignments home and will prefer to keep the notebooks in their lockers, while others will prefer to keep their assignments at home. When you first hand out the forms, you can talk to students about what they would like to do to protect their privacy.

Ending the Group

By the tenth lesson, the SSET group normally feels safe, and trusting relationships have formed within the group. Thus, the prospect of the group ending can be difficult for students and SSET leaders alike. The final lesson focuses on ending the group and looking to the future. However, students often raise the following question:

"If I have a problem, can I come and talk to you about it?"

Here is a suitable answer:

"You need to consider me from here on out as a regular teacher/school counselor, not your SSET group leader. Once SSET is over, you can come to me with problems just like you talk to other teachers/school counselors about problems, but if you need more help than that, I will probably suggest that you talk to [name of clinical backup]."

It is important for SSET leaders to end the group and not to encourage students to continue any kind of "special" relationship with them. As a general rule, **after the SSET group ends, you should treat former group members as you would treat any other students in the school.**

However, some students might need additional support beyond the end of the groups. If there are other programs running at the school, you can consider whether the student might benefit from them. In some cases, a referral for professional help may be appropriate. Consultation with the project's clinical backup at the end of groups is a good idea to ensure that all students will get the support they need after the group ends.

Scenarios: What to Do When You Can't Think of an Example

If you have difficulty thinking of an example of a stressful situation, the list below may help you. While it is always preferable to use examples relevant to the students in your group, you can always use one of the following examples if you have trouble thinking of something more personal:

1. You failed a test.
2. One of your friends tells you that your boyfriend/girlfriend was talking to another girl/boy.
3. You have to walk in late to a class.
4. You come home and you can tell that your mom is drunk.
5. Your parents are yelling loudly at one another or physically hitting one another.
6. You see two people sitting near you in class passing notes back and forth.
7. You have to give a speech/book report in front of class.
8. You don't understand something in class.
9. Your mother is 15 minutes late to pick you up from school.
10. You are at home alone and hear a loud noise outside.
11. Bullies in the hall on the way to third period always taunt you.
12. You have to sleep away from home.
13. You forgot your homework assignment.
14. You are invited to a birthday party at the park, but you're afraid of going to that park.
15. You want to ask someone to go to a school dance with you.
16. Another student asks to copy your homework or cheat off of you during a test.
17. You are having trouble sleeping by yourself.
18. You get called to the principal or dean's office.
19. Your mom says she wants to have a talk with you after school.
20. You lose your favorite notebook and you see a classmate with the same one.

LESSON PLANS

Lisa H. Jaycox
Audra K. Langley

Lesson One: Introduction

1.	Introduce Agenda for the Session	4.	Why We Are Here: Our Stories
2.	Introduction to the Group	5.	Plan for Independent Practice
3.	Explanation of SSET	6.	Review

Overall Goal

Build trust and group cohesion while giving students information about what to expect in the group.

Student Objectives

1. Students will increase in their trust for one another and their group leader.
2. Students will verbalize the reason for attending the support group.
3. Students will increase in their comfort in the group.
4. Students will know what to expect from the group.

Materials

1. A bag of M&M candies or similar multicolored candy.
2. A confidentiality statement (for example, the "Confidentiality Contract," p. 128) to be signed by all group members.
3. Index cards (with prewritten questions for the M&M Game).
4. Copies of the "Why I Am Here" worksheet (p. 130).
5. Copies of the "Goals" worksheet (pp. 131–132).
6. Copies of the "Letter to Parents" (p. 133), personalized with your name and contact information.
7. "Return to Class" slips (filled out).

Leader Preparation

1. Interview each student privately to confirm trauma exposure, problems, and desire to attend the group.
2. Obtain parent permission.
3. Agree with each student on how he or she will present trauma to the group; secure permission to say it for him or her if it proves to be more difficult than expected.
4. Locate private space for group meetings.
5. Create a schedule for all ten group meetings.

6. Review "Disclosure by Group Members" (pp. 29–30) and Table L1.1, Suggestions for Troubleshooting the Why We Are Here Exercise (p. 59).

7. Review "The Dos and Don'ts of the M&M Game" (p. 129).

8. Write out introductory questions on index cards for easy use during the M&M Game.

9. Personalize the "Letter to Parents" that will be sent home with your signature; include your contact information if you can supply a way for parents to reach you.

Procedures/Teaching

1. Introduce Agenda for Session

Welcome students to the support group and briefly review what will happen in today's lesson.

> *"I would like to start by welcoming you all to this support group. You are all here today because you've been through something very stressful. This group is designed to help you with that experience and to help you move on from it. Today, I'll begin by describing our meeting schedule and how we'll protect each other's privacy. Then we'll spend some time getting to know each other a little bit. I'll explain what the group is about and we'll each say why we're here. At the end, I'll give you an assignment to do at home and bring to the next group meeting."*

2. Introduction to the Group

a. Review the Meeting Schedule

Review the meeting schedule and pass out written schedules for the students to take home. Talk about the importance of being on time to show respect for other group members and to review their between-lesson practices. Make sure that group members understand that each lesson builds on the one before it and that it is important to make it to all of the lessons.

b. Review the Concept of Confidentiality

Review the concept of confidentiality and elicit from group members reasons why they might want the group to be private. Request that group members keep everything that is talked about in the group private, but allow group members to talk about their own participation with anyone they want. Review a few examples to make sure that everyone understands. Here are some examples you can use:

> *"Let's say that there is a boy named Joe in this group. If Joe were to tell everyone in the group that he has been fighting a lot with his brother, would it be okay to tell a classmate at school that he said that? Why or why not?"*

> *"Would it be okay to tell a classmate at school who the others in the group are and why they are in the group? Why or why not?"*

> *"If I feel upset after the group, would it be okay for me to tell my mother what it was that made me upset? Why or why not?"*

It may be a good idea to have group members sign a statement (for example, the "Confidentiality Contract") saying that they will keep what others say in the group private to ensure that they are taking this issue seriously.

Engagement Activity

Play the the M&M Game[1] with the students. (Be sure to review "The Dos and Don'ts of the M&M Game" before the lesson.) To play the M&M Game, pass around a bag of M&M candies and tell each student to take a small handful but not to eat them. Tell them that you are going to ask them some questions about themselves and that everyone who has a certain color M&M in their hand has to answer the question in front of the group before they can eat it. For example,

> *"This is for anyone who has a blue M&M: What do you do for fun after school?"*

Model an appropriate answer yourself first and play along so that they can get to know you as well. If the students have more than one blue M&M, they must tell you one thing for each one. Other possible questions include

> *"What kind of job would you like to have after you finish school?"*
>
> *"What sports or physical activities are you good at?"*
>
> *"When do you have fun during the school day?"*

Write questions on index cards before the lesson for easy use during the game. You can then give one of the students an index card and ask him or her to read the question aloud to increase group participation.

The goals of this game are to build group rapport and to get the group members used to sharing personal information. Try to use questions that will be relevant and interesting to the group (depending on age, gender, maturity, etc.), but avoid questions that will lead to too much self-disclosure at this early stage in the group. (See "The Dos and Don'ts of the M&M Game.")

3. Explanation of SSET

Give an overview of the idea that thoughts and behaviors influence the way we feel. Draw a triangle on the board. Write the phrase "Stress/Trauma/Violence" to one side, with an arrow pointing at the triangle (see Figure 1.1 on the next page). Then say,

> *"What do I mean by stress? Trauma? Violence? Can you give some examples of things that might happen that would be stressful? That would be a trauma? That would be violence?"*

Elicit ideas about stressful events and list them under the "Stress/Trauma/ Violence" heading. Then ask,

> *"When something stressful happens, such as [use one of their examples], how does that change what we think? What we do? What we feel?"*

---

[1]   This game was modified from one originally used in Gillham, J., Jaycox, L. H., Reivich, K. J., Seligam, M. E. P., & Silver, T. (1991). Manual for Leaders of the Coping Skills Program for Children. Unpublished manual. Copyright Foresight, Inc.

Figure L1.1—Stress/Trauma/Violence Triangle

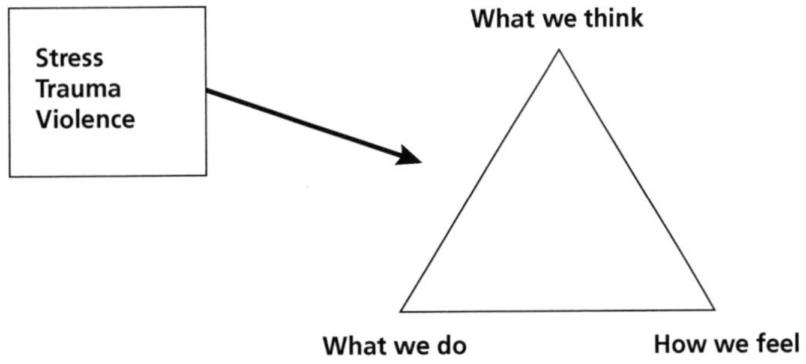

Make the point that stress or trauma causes all three aspects (thoughts, actions, and feelings) to change and that each then impacts the others, making feelings worsen. Here's an example:

"You get into a car accident. That's the stress or trauma. Afterward, you feel shaky, nervous, upset. You think that driving is really dangerous, and you don't want to go in the car again. When your mother asks if you want to go shopping with her, you say no and stay home because you don't want to be in the car."

Using a made-up name in this example can be useful. As the group progresses, you can refer back to the named person when explaining what you are working on. For instance, Lesson Three could be introduced this way:

"Remember George, who was in that car accident? Remember how George thought about what happened to him? Well, today, we're going to work on changing that kind of thinking."

Next, explain how SSET is going to help the students cope with upsetting things.

"You are all here because you had something really traumatic, stressful, or violent happen to you. In this program, we are going to work on all three corners of the triangle. We are going to

- *learn some exercises that will make you **feel** better, and less nervous or upset*
- *learn some ways to **think** about things that will help you feel better*
- *learn some ways to **do** things so that you are able to do everything you want to be able to do and not feel upset when you do it."*

4. Why We Are Here: Our Stories

This activity will be used to describe the stress or trauma that brought each student into the group. Hand out the "Why I Am Here" worksheet. Begin with this explanation:

"We're going to spend a few minutes talking about the biggest stress or trauma each of you went through, the one that brought you into the group. It can sometimes be upsetting to talk about stresses or traumas, and we don't want you to feel upset today. So please just share a very little

bit of what happened to you so that the others in the group have an idea, but not so much that you start to feel upset about it.

"If anyone wants help from me in telling the group what happened, let me know, and I'll say it for you.

"If more than one thing happened to you, tell us about the different things and which one bothers you the most now.

"Take a look at the worksheet I gave you and spend a minute or two filling in what you want to say to the group. I'll come around the room and help any of you that want help. I'll read the sections out loud [read headings out loud]."

Spend a minute or two allowing each group member to write down his or her plan for telling the group, and then allow each member to tell the others about the event or events that brought him or her into the group.

For those with more than one event, ask them to tell the group which one bothers them the most at present. If a student says that all are equal, ask which one was the most difficult at the time that it happened. Take notes about the relevant trauma for each student so that you can refer to them during the program.

It is important to limit disclosure during this exercise to just a few sentences, yet it is equally important to get all students to share something. The description should stick to the facts of what happened (what, when, where, who) and can be anything from a few words (for example, "I'm here because I saw a friend get shot in a drive-by") to a few sentences (for example, "I was walking home from school and some guys came out of an alley. At first I didn't know what was happening, but then they came toward me and I knew they wanted something. They took my watch and my money and beat me up"). Some suggestions for troubleshooting this exercise are found in Table L1.1 on the next page.

At the end, summarize the kinds of experiences for the group, emphasizing commonalities. For instance,

"This shows us that everyone has had something really stressful happen. Every one of you had a different thing happen, and it seems like a few/several/all of you went through

- *something that was very scary*
- *a situation in which someone might have been hurt*
- *something really startling or shocking*
- *a situation in which you didn't have any control over what happened.*

"We're going to work on making these stresses or traumas easier for you to deal with."

5. Plan for Independent Practice

Ask students to pull out their group lesson activity entitled "Goals." Describe the activities assignment of setting goals for the support group. Read through the steps of the worksheet with them and have the students begin to work on it if there is time. Tell them to share their worksheets with their parents and ask a parent to complete the bottom section. Ask them bring the worksheets to the next group lesson.

Ask the students to give your letter to their parents and have a parent sign it and fill it out. Remind the students to return the form next time.

Spend a few minutes asking to students to plan where to keep their worksheets and SSET materials and how to maintain the privacy of these documents.

Table L1.1—Suggestions for Troubleshooting the Why We Are Here Exercise

Problem	How the Leader Can Help
Student will not fill out the form, says he or she does not want to share	Remind students that it is a group about moving on from the trauma and that sharing is an important part of that.
	Offer to say what happened to the student for him or her as planned in the individual meeting before the group began.
	On the student's turn, say, *"[Student name] does not feel comfortable sharing this yet, but gave me permission to say it for him/her. What happened is ___. [Student], did I get that right? Did you want to add anything to what I said?"*
Student fills out the form but freezes when called upon	Say, *"I know it can be hard to share this. Why don't you try just reading what you have written there?"*
	If that doesn't work, say *"Can I read it for you?"*
	If that doesn't work, revert to saying it for the student, as outlined above.
Student begins to tell the group too many details, going beyond the sentences written down or what has been agreed on	Say, *"Okay, [student name], I think that gives the group a good idea of what happened to you. We're going to have more time to talk about these things later on in the group, and we'll work on it a lot in Lessons Six and Seven. Today we want to keep it kind of short, so no one starts to feel overwhelmed. I think that's good for today. Thanks for sharing that."*

6. Review

Briefly review what happened in the group, then preview the next session.

"Today we set out to introduce the group and ourselves to each other. By now you should all know what this group is about, and you should know a little bit about each other. You also should know all about how the confidentiality will work in the group. Next time, we'll begin to work on some relaxation skills, and we'll talk about how people commonly react to traumatic or stressful events."

> **Parent phone call**
> Call parents if possible to introduce yourself and to remind them of what to expect. Letters are sent home after this lesson in case phone calls are not possible.

Lesson Two: Common Reactions to Trauma and Strategies for Relaxation

L2

1.	Introduce Agenda for the Session	4.	Relaxation to Combat Anxiety
2.	Independent Practice Review	5.	Plan for Independent Practice
3.	Education About Common Reactions to Trauma	6.	Review

Overall Goal

Teach students about the normal or common problems that we have after a traumatic experience. Teach them one skill (relaxation) that they can use to calm anxiety.

Student Objectives

1. Students will increase understanding about negative thoughts, feelings, and actions that resulted from their experience with stress/trauma/violence.
2. Students will feel more "normal" as a result of understanding commonalities in reactions to trauma.
3. Students will have hope that the support group will help them reduce some of the negative thoughts, feelings, and actions related to their experience.
4. Students will have a sense of support from their peers in the group.
5. Students will experience increased communication and support from their parents.
6. Students will learn how to relax their bodies.

Materials

1. Index cards and a hat (optional).
2. Copies of the "List of Problems People Have After Stress" (p. 136) and highlighters (optional).
3. Copies of the "Information About Common Reactions to Stress or Trauma" worksheet (pp. 137–138).
4. Copies of the "Activities" worksheet (p. 139).
5. "Return to Class" slips (filled out).

Leader Preparation

1. Review information about students' problems related to the stress/trauma/violence so that you can elicit discussion from them and others on the most salient issues.
2. Prepare index cards with a problem written on each one if you plan to use that method of guiding the discussion.
3. Respond to parent questions/concerns if possible by phone or in writing.

Procedures/Teaching

1.   Introduce Agenda for Session

Welcome students to the support group and briefly review what will happen in today's lesson.

"Welcome back to the group. Today, we'll begin reviewing your "Goals" worksheet that I handed out last week. Then we'll discuss common reactions to stressful or traumatic events, and each of you will be able to talk about the kinds of problems you've been having. Then we'll do a relaxation exercise together to teach you some ways that you can relax your body. At the end, I'll give you an assignment to do at home and to bring into the next group."

2.   Independent Practice Review

Review each group member's "Goals" worksheet by asking for volunteers to share their goals. Reassure group members that goals are attainable and remind them of the ways in which you will help them with each goal. At the same time, point out which goals are unrealistic and help group members understand how they can begin working on some goals in group lessons and then continue to work on them on their own afterward. The overall tone of this part of the lesson should convey a realistic, hopeful attitude. Examples follow in Table L2.1.

If some group members did not have their parents complete the worksheet or did not want to share it with their parents, normalize that for them ("Yes, parents can be busy, and it can be hard to get this done" or "Yes, sometimes these things feel too private to share with others"). This will help ensure that they are not embarrassed in front of the group.

Table L2.1—Suggested Leader Responses to Stated Goals

Stated Goal	Suggested Leader Response
Do more of the things I used to do (checks box next to this on worksheet)	*"Great. We're going to be working on that in the group. I think that's a goal for a lot of people."*
Writes in: Sleep better	*"We'll talk about how common sleep problems are later today. And this is something that should get better as the group goes on—we have a few different ways to help you with that. We'll start the first one today when we practice relaxation."*
Writes in: Do better in school	*"That's a good goal. We can help with some parts of that, like helping you concentrate better and helping you sleep better. But you'll have to study too!"*
Writes in: Get along with my mom	*"Has that been more of a problem since [the event]? If so, we can work on that. We can help you communicate better with your mom about the kinds of problems you've been having, and in the last few sessions, we'll be working on how to solve problems that you are having with others."*

3.   Education About Common Reactions to Trauma

Take some time to convey information about general types of problems that students experience when they have been exposed to traumatic life events. You will lead a discussion here. There are three goals for this discussion:

- Normalize problems and make students see that these are reasonable ways to react to extreme stress. (For example, say "After something bad happens to you, it makes sense to be prepared for another bad thing to happen, or to feel 'on guard.'")
- Explain how the support group will help them with these sorts of problems. (For example, say "We're going to learn some relaxation skills in this group to help you with those feelings of anxiety or nervousness.")
- Build support among group members. (For example, say "I can see that a lot of you have been having trouble sleeping.")

In this discussion format, remember that you do not need to cover all the material. Take one of the student worksheets and use it to guide your discussion, crossing off items as they get discussed. Try to cover the topics with some breadth, but do not feel the need to be exhaustive or to describe each kind of problem in depth. Once the majority of topics are covered, scan your list to see if any important ones have been left out of the discussion. If so, introduce them.

If group members add additional problems to the list, adopt an accepting attitude and try to make the connections to the traumatic events. If there are no apparent connections, gently remind the group members that there are all sorts of problems, but only those that stem from stress and trauma will be discussed in the group. Since the goal is to normalize problems, an inclusive discussion that includes all sorts of problems is best. For example, if a student describes completely panicking or "freaking out" about something (a reaction that is not on the list), reflect back the extreme anxiety and how common it is to experience anxiety of all types following trauma. Adding comments to the group members' experiences (examples follow) will help to normalize the problem and provide hope that such problems can be reduced in the group.

Engagement Activity

During the discussion, pause at each problem and ask students to highlight the parts that apply to themselves.

In groups of middle school or high school students, pass out colored highlighter pens and ask group members to turn to the list of common reactions in the "List of Problems People Have After Stress." Ask them to highlight the problems they have been having, then lead the discussion below.

In a group of elementary school or middle school students, write the problems on slips of paper or index cards and put them in a hat. Have each group member pick a problem and describe what it's like for him or her. Have other group members add their experiences as well, and then move on to another group member.

Having nightmares or trouble sleeping.

When something really scary or upsetting happens, it takes a while to figure out exactly what happened and what it means. After severe stress or trauma, people tend to keep thinking about what happened in order to "digest" it, just like your stomach has to work to digest a big meal. This can take a long time. Nightmares are one way of digesting what happened to you.

Thinking about it all the time.

This is another way to digest what happened. Just like having nightmares, thinking about the trauma all the time is a problem because it makes you feel upset. It can be unpleasant.

Wanting to NOT think or talk about it.

This is natural, since it is upsetting to think about a past stress or trauma, and doing so can make you feel all sorts of emotions. Avoiding it makes things easier, but only for a little while. It's important to digest what happened sooner or later. So, while avoiding it sometimes makes sense, you have to set aside some time to digest it also. This group can be the time and place you set aside to digest what happened to you.

Avoiding places, people, or things that make you think about it.

Just like not wanting to talk about or think about the trauma, avoiding situations that remind you of what happened can help you feel better right then. The problem with this, though, is that it keeps you from doing normal things that are an important part of your life. The goal of this group is to get you back to the point where you are able to do whatever you want to do without worrying about whether it will remind you of what happened.

Feeling scared for no reason.

Sometimes this happens because you remember what happened to you or because you are thinking about what happened. Other times it happens because your body is so tense all the time that you just start feeling scared. Either way, we can work on helping you feel calmer when it happens.

Feeling "crazy" or out of control.

If a lot of these common reactions are problems for you, you can start to feel really out of control or even crazy. Don't worry, though; these problems don't mean that you are going crazy. They are all normal reactions to stress or trauma, and there are ways to help you feel better.

Not being able to remember parts of what happened.

This happens to a lot of people. The stressful event can be so awful that your memory doesn't work the way it usually does. Sometimes it gets easier to remember later on, and sometimes it gets harder. This can be frustrating, but it is really normal.

Having trouble concentrating at school or at home.

With all the nervousness you are feeling and all the time you are spending thinking about what happened, it can be hard to concentrate on schoolwork or even on what your friends or family say to you.

L2

Being on guard to protect yourself; feeling like something bad is about to happen.

After something bad happens to you, it makes sense to be prepared for another bad thing to happen. The problem with this is that you can spend so much time waiting for the next bad thing to happen that you don't have time or energy for other things in your life. Also, it is scary to think something bad is going to happen.

Jumping when there is a loud noise.

This is one way that your body says it is prepared for action in case something else happens. As you begin to feel calmer, this will go away.

Feeling anger.

Some people feel angry about the stress or trauma that happened, or about the things that happened afterward. Other people just feel angry all the time, at everything and everybody. Both of these are normal and will get better as you begin to digest what happened to you.

Feeling shame.

Sometimes people are ashamed about what happened to them or how they acted. Even though it's hard to believe, this gets better the more that you talk about what happened. If you keep it a secret, it's hard for the shame to go away.

Feeling guilt.

People can feel guilty about what happened or about something they did or did not do. Sometimes you blame yourself for things that you couldn't control. You may also feel guilty for upsetting your parents. Guilty feelings can make it hard to talk about what happened.

Feeling sadness/grief/loss.

Sometimes stress events or traumas include losing someone close to you or losing something that is important to you. This makes you feel sad and down. We'll help you talk about these feelings in the group.

Feeling bad about yourself.

Sometimes, all this stress can make you feel really bad about yourself, like you're a bad person or that no one likes you. This makes it harder to be friendly and to have fun with others.

Having physical health problems and complaints.

Stress has an effect on your body as well. People sometimes get sick more often or notice pain and discomfort more often when they have been under stress.

At the end of the discussion, summarize for the group that people feel many different things but that most of these reactions are normal. Use the information gleaned during this discussion to guide the program for each individual group member, focusing practice of relevant techniques on the group members who need that technique the most.

L2

4.   Relaxation Training to Combat Anxiety

The goal of this part of the lesson is to train group members in progressive muscle relaxation. Present the following rationale:

"We've just reviewed some of the many problems that are common after you have gone though a traumatic experience. Many of these problems are ones that make your bodies more alert or tense. Stress makes our bodies tense, and feeling nervous or upset makes it even worse. But there are ways to relax your body that will make you feel calmer. Today, I'll teach you one way to do that."

Engagement Activity

Ask group members to lean back in their chairs (or lie on the floor if that is more comfortable), close their eyes, and follow your instructions. Giggling is common among students doing relaxation exercises. Warn them that they might find it funny at first, but that they should try to relax and concentrate on your voice. If group members have trouble staying focused, move over to them one by one and put your hand on their shoulder to help them focus. (If, however, the group member is jumpy, warn him or her that you will touch a shoulder before you do it.) Guide the students:

"I'd like you to start by thinking of some place that makes you really comfortable, like your bed or the bathtub or the couch or the beach. Imagine that you are lying down there or sitting comfortably. Take a breath in [wait 3–4 seconds] and out [wait 3–4 seconds], in . . . and out . . . in . . . and out. Try to keep breathing this way as we continue. And keep thinking about your most comfortable spot.

"Now I'd like you to make a fist and squeeze it really tight. You can open your eyes and see how I'm doing it if you're not sure how. Hold it. Now relax it completely and shake it out. Do it again; make a fist. Now relax it completely. Can you feel the difference between how it was when it was tight and now how it feels when it's relaxed? Let's do the same thing for the rest of your arms. Tighten up your whole arm, like you are making a muscle, and hold it. Now relax it completely. Do it again. Tighten, now relax. Now let's move to your shoulders. Bring your shoulders up to your ears and tighten them . . . hold it. Now relax. Do that again. Bring your shoulders way up near your ears . . . hold it . . . now relax them completely. Make sure your hands, arms, and shoulders are completely relaxed. Breathe in . . . and out . . . in . . . and out.

"Let's work on your face now. Scrunch up your face as tight as you can, close your eyes tight, scrunch up your mouth, and hold it. Now relax. Try that again. Tighten up your whole face and hold it. Now relax it. Keep breathing like we did before . . . in . . . and out . . . in . . . and out.

> **Implementation tip**
> To lessen the possibility of giggling or talking, you can turn chairs so that they face outward from the circle instead of inward.

"Next comes your body. Arch your back as much as you can and put your shoulders way back, like I am doing. Hold it. Now relax that. Next, lean forward onto your knees, curl your back the other way, and tighten up your stomach as much as you can. Hold it. Now relax it. Do that again . . . hold it, and relax it. Keep breathing . . . in . . . and out . . . in . . . and out.

"Let's work on your legs and feet. Straighten your legs up in the air in front of you and bring your toes as close to your face as you can. Tighten up your bottom also. Now hold it. Relax. Do that again . . . hold it, and now relax. Next, point your toes as far as you can away from your face, and again tighten up your leg muscles. Hold it. Now relax. Do that again . . . hold it, and relax. Breathe in . . . and out . . . in . . . and out.

"Think about all the parts of your body and relax any part that is tight now. Let all the tension go out of your body. Breathe in . . . and out . . . in . . . and out. Now begin to open your eyes, sit back up, and be a part of the group again."

5. Plan for Independent Practice

Give group members copies of the "Information About Common Reactions to Stress or Trauma" and ask them to talk with their parents about the problems bothering them.

Tell group members to practice the relaxation exercise before bed three times before the next group meeting.

Distribute copies of the "Activities" worksheet. Ask the students to fill them out and bring them to the next meeting.

6. Review

Briefly review what happened in the group, then preview the next session.

"Today we set out to talk about common reactions to traumatic events and to learn a relaxation skill. Next time, we'll start to talk about our thinking and how we can make sure we're not making ourselves more upset than we need to be."

Lesson Three: Thoughts and Feelings

1. Introduce Agenda for the Session
2. Independent Practice Review
3. Fear Thermometer
4. Examples of Thoughts Affecting Feelings
5. Linkage Between Thoughts and Feelings
6. Plan for Independent Practice
7. Review

L3

Overall Goal

Teach students a common language to describe their level of feelings and to teach them that their thoughts can fuel their feelings. Introduce a skill for challenging their unrealistic thoughts with helpful thoughts.

Student Objectives

1. Students will increase their ability to observe their own thoughts.
2. Students will increase their ability to challenge thoughts that are getting in their way.
3. Students will experience less anxiety by decreasing some of their unrealistic thinking and increasing helpful thinking.

Materials

1. Copies of the "Fear Thermometers" worksheet (pp. 142–145).
2. Comic strips, video clips, or other examples that demonstrate how thoughts affect feelings.
3. Copies of the "Noticing Your Thoughts and Feelings" worksheet (p. 146).
4. "Return to Class" slips (filled out).

Leader Preparation

1. Review common underlying problematic thoughts (e.g., the world is a dangerous place, I am incompetent) and how they may apply to what you already know about group members. (See "Why Do We Address Thoughts in Trauma Survivors?" p. 13.)
2. For demonstrative purposes, have relevant examples ready of problematic situations, particularly those situations that might be seen as an "overreaction" from an outsider.

Procedures/Teaching

1.   Introduce Agenda for Session

Welcome students back to the group and briefly review what will happen in today's lesson.

"Welcome back to the group. Today we will begin by discussing your relaxation practice and how it went with sharing the handout with your parents. Then we'll learn a way to help describe how we are feeling. Then we will talk about our thoughts, and how they make us feel certain ways. At the end, I'll give you an assignment to do at home and bring back to the next group."

2.   Independent Practice Review

Review group members' progress with the relaxation technique and help them solve any problems, as seen in Table L3.1.

Table L3.1—How the Leader Can Help Solve Relaxation Problems

Problem	How the Leader Can Help
Not enough time/too noisy in the house	Ask the group member to talk to a parent to figure out a way to have quiet time set aside for the relaxation exercise.
Couldn't relax—kept thinking about problems	Ask the group member to continue to practice and to make sure that he or she is doing the exercise correctly. Review the relaxation technique for the whole group if necessary. Another option is to record tapes of the instructions.
Felt worse/made me upset	In some rare cases, relaxation can have the opposite effect and make people feel agitated or panicky. If this seems true for an individual in the group, ask him or her to stop using the technique and to try to identify or explore other ways to relax at home.

Ask group members if they shared "Information About Common Reactions to Stress or Trauma" with their parents and how that went. If group members did not complete the activity, ask them to explain why not. Use this opportunity to remind group members about the rationale.

"Though it may be embarrassing to admit that you are having any problems, these kinds of problems are really common, and your parents can help you with it if they know what is happening to you."

"Though it is hard to talk and think about what happened to you, part of being in this group involves digesting that experience, and the more you take advantage of opportunities to do that, the quicker you will feel better."

3.   Fear Thermometer

Use the Fear Thermometer concept (see Figure L3.1) to introduce a way for group members to talk about how anxious or nervous they feel in various situations.

"Today we're going to talk about feelings and thinking, but in order to do that, we need to find some way to measure how we are feeling. Who can tell me how we measure the temperature outside? We can use the same idea for measuring how scared or upset we feel. We call it the Fear Thermometer."

Show the children the first Fear Thermometer. Use the other Fear Thermometers to show different levels of feelings and ask group members to give examples of when they felt each way (not at all scared or upset; a little scared or upset; pretty scared or upset; really scared or upset).

Figure L3.1—Fear Thermometers

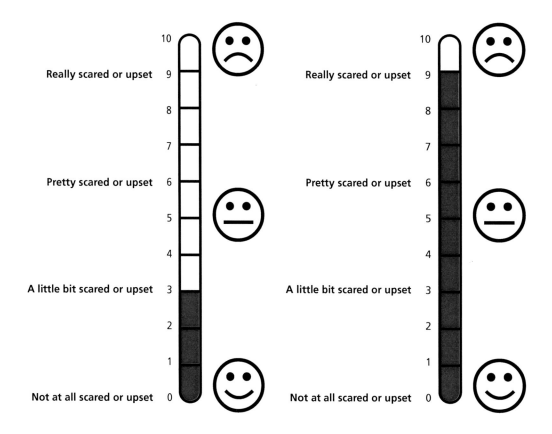

Explain that the "10" on the Fear Thermometer is kept for those times when we are completely and utterly scared and upset. Tell group members that they will be using the Fear Thermometer to tell how they feel during the rest of the group lessons.

Engagement Activity

Give each student a copy of a blank Fear Thermometer. Ask the students to think of a time that they felt relaxed and were enjoying themselves (some examples are on the couch watching their favorite TV show, reading a good book, listening to their favorite music with a friend, at a fun family party or get together). Have the students assign a Fear Thermometer rating for how they are feeling "right now" in the group as they are imagining or talking about this situation (not when the particular event was occurring).

Next, have the students think of a time when they felt worried, nervous, or stressed out (some examples are before a big test, a book report, or speech in front of the class; taking a report card home to their parents). Have the students assign a Fear Thermometer rating for how they are feeling "right now" in the group as they are imagining or talking about this situation (not when the particular event was occurring).

Ask the students to write in real events in their lives next to some of the ratings to provide "anchors." For instance, they can write "lying on the beach" next to the "0" rating, "waiting for the math test to be handed out" next to a "5," and "when the trauma happened" next to a "10" on the Fear Thermometer. Make sure that they are all using the scale correctly. (Query any extreme ratings to make sure that the child would actually feel that way/was actually feeling that way during the event).

4. Examples of Thoughts Affecting Feelings

The goal of this part of the lesson is to show that thoughts can cause and fuel feelings. Begin with an example of the way thoughts can influence feelings.

"Does anyone know the story of Chicken Little? How does that go? [Fill in story details as necessary.] Chicken Little was scratching around in the barnyard, and then suddenly felt something hit him in the head. He thought to himself, 'The sky is falling!' He was so certain that the sky was falling that he ran all over the place yelling, 'The sky is falling, the sky is falling!' and everyone thought he was crazy. He was probably feeling about a '9' on the Fear Thermometer. Was the sky really falling? No. An acorn had fallen off the tree and hit Chicken Little on the head. So he had gotten all upset about nothing—just a little acorn.

*"In this situation, Chicken Little's **thoughts** got him into a lot of trouble and made him all upset. Even worse, his thoughts were not true—the sky was not really falling. What would have happened if Chicken Little had thought, 'An acorn just hit me on the head!'? Would he have felt as scared or upset? No, he would probably have just kept on scratching around the barnyard without feeling scared or upset.*

"Today, we are going to talk about how all of us sometimes have thoughts that are unhelpful and sometimes untrue. We are going to talk about the way that you can double check to make sure that you aren't getting upset over nothing or keeping yourself from doing things because you are afraid."

Engagement Activity

Use comic strips or TV/video clips (e.g., SpongeBob SquarePants or other relevant sitcoms or cartoons) and allow kids to identify thoughts and feelings in the situation and how the situation would differ if the thoughts involved changed.

5. Linkage Between Thoughts and Feelings

The goal of this part of the lesson is to make sure that group members understand the way in which thoughts and feelings are linked. Pick an example that is relevant to the group (use one of the group member's own problem situations, if possible) to do the following exercise:

"Different kinds of thoughts can lead to different feelings. Let's take an example and list possible feelings that someone might have in that situation."

Engagement Activity

Example 1

"You are walking through the cafeteria at school, and a bunch of kids are laughing and looking over at you."

Create a column entitled "Feelings" on the chalkboard or whiteboard and have group members come up with possible feelings to add to the list. Examples include angry, sad, embarrassed, fine, good.

Note that students often will come up with the negative emotions easily but will forget to include feeling "okay" or "good" on this list. If they do this, you should add these feelings to the list.

"What are some ways that you might feel if this happened to you?"

List feelings, eliciting several different types, on the board.

"So, this is interesting. We have the same situation, but it's causing all kinds of different feelings. Why is this? Let's take a look at the way that you might be thinking about this situation that would lead to the different feelings."

Next, create a column to the right of the "Feelings" entitled "Thoughts" and help the group come up with thoughts that may be leading to the various emotions. Make the point that different thoughts lead to different feelings, even if the situation is exactly the same.

"What might you be saying to yourself that would make you feel ___?"

Write feelings and possible thoughts in two columns on the board as in the example table below.

Feelings	Possible Thoughts
Angry	They have no right to laugh at me!
Sad	No one likes me. I'll never have good friends like that.
Embarrassed	They must think I look funny.
Okay	They're just telling jokes; it's not about me.
Good	They think I'm funny and like me.

Follow these same steps with examples generated from the group. If the group is unable to come up with examples, here is another example you can prompt them with.

Example 2

"You are waiting for your brother/sister outside of a store, and some kids come up and start to hassle you."

Feelings	Possible Thoughts
Angry	They have no right to laugh at me!
Sad	No one likes me. I'll never have good friends like that.
Embarrassed	They must think I look funny.
Okay	They're just telling jokes; it's not about me.
Good	They think I'm funny and like me.

L3

6. Plan for Independent Practice

Distribute copies of the Fear Thermometer and of the "Noticing Your Thoughts and Feelings" worksheet. Describe the assignment, which is to practice observing thoughts and feelings at home. Give group members several copies of the worksheet and have them practice with an example before they leave the group if there is enough time. Try to give group members specific instructions about the kinds of situations to work on, depending on their needs. Emphasize that feelings can be positive or negative.

7. Review

Briefly review what happened in the group, then preview the next session.

"Today we began to notice how thoughts can affect the way that we feel. The important thing to remember is that our thoughts are not always true, and they can sometimes get us into trouble because they make us more upset than we need to be. Its important to make sure your thoughts are accurate, or true. We're going to keep working on this next week, and we will do a fun exercise called the 'Hot Seat' to help you practice how to come up with thoughts that are more realistic or help you solve the problem you are having."

Lesson Four: Helpful Thinking

1. Introduce Agenda for the Session	4. Hot Seat: What Will Happen Next
2. Independent Practice Review	5. Plan for Independent Practice
3. Hot Seat: Check the Facts	6. Review

Overall Goal

Teach students to challenge their negative thoughts and replace them with more-helpful thoughts.

Student Objectives

1. Students will increase their ability to challenge thoughts that are getting in their way.
2. Students will increase their ability to generate helpful thoughts.
3. Students will experience less anxiety as a result of mastering these skills.

Materials

1. An extra chair to designate as the Hot Seat.
2. Copies of the "Questions You Can Use to Argue Against Negative Thoughts" worksheet (p. 150).
3. Copies of the "Hot Seat Exercise" worksheet (pp. 151–152).
4. "Return to Class" slips (filled out).

Leader Preparation

1. Have scenarios relevant to the group members prepared to use as examples during the Hot Seat activity in case students are unable to generate their own.
2. Read the "The Dos and Don'ts of the Hot Seat Activity" (pp. 148–149).

Procedures/Teaching

1. Introduce Agenda for the Session

Welcome students back to the group and briefly review what will happen in today's lesson.

"Welcome back to the group. We'll start by reviewing the activities from last time, to see how you are doing in questioning your own thoughts. Today we are going to do a fun activity that is called the 'Hot Seat.' In the Hot Seat, we'll learn ways to come up with helpful thoughts and try to all get better and faster at questioning our own thoughts. At the end, I'll give you a new assignment to do at home to bring back to the next group."

2. Independent Practice Review

Review the activities from the previous lesson.

"Let's review the negative and helpful thoughts that each of you were able to come up with in your take-home practice."

Look for the trouble spots listed in Table L4.1 and correct them as needed.

Table L4.1—How the Leader Can Help Solve Problems with Noticing Thoughts and Feelings

Problem	How the Leader Can Help
Didn't do any activities	Attempt to find out why and suggest ways to improve compliance. Ask if the group member noticed any negative thinking in the past week and to describe what it was. Ask if he or she challenged that negative thinking in any way. If so, praise him or her for work well done. If not, ask the child to try to do it right then and to ask for help from other group members.
Didn't have any problems or negative thoughts	Ask the group member to think of past experiences if nothing went wrong in the prior week.

3. Hot Seat: Check the Facts[1]

The goal of this part of the lesson is to teach group members to challenge their negative thinking when it is unrealistic or unhelpful and replace it with helpful thoughts.

"How can you argue with negative thoughts? When you have a very negative thought, or a really strong reaction to something, it's worth considering whether another way of thinking about it might be more helpful. We owe it to ourselves to come up with a thought that helps us by

- *being more accurate (true) than the negative thought*
- *making us feel better when we think about it that way*
- *helping us plan what to do next.*

---

[1] This exercise was originally developed for use in depression prevention in children in Gillham, J., Jaycox, L. H., Reivich, K. J., Seligman, M. E. P., Silver, T. (1991). Manual for Leaders of the Coping Skills Program for Children. Unpublished manual. Copyright Foresight, Inc. The exercise was subsequently modified in a similar fashion for adolescents in Asarnow, J., Jaycox, L. H., Clarke, G., Lewinsohn, P., Hops, H., Rohde, P. (1999). Stress and Your Mood: A Manual. Los Angeles: UCLA School of Medicine.

*"We call all of these **"helpful thoughts"** because they help us feel better or move on with solving the problem instead of just feeling bad."*

Engagement Activity

"Let's take an example."

Create two columns entitled "Negative Thoughts" and "Helpful Thoughts" on the chalkboard or whiteboard.

Example 1

"You take a math test and it is much harder than you expected. You have not studied enough. When you get it back, you see that you got a 63 on it out of 100, a D. You think to yourself, 'I'm going get a bad grade in math!' and 'My parents are going to be so mad at me.'"

Write these thoughts down on the board under the "Negative Thoughts" column. Hand out and refer students to the list of questions to help them generate Hot Seat thoughts (also listed below).

List of Hot Seat Questions

Questions about how true or accurate the thought is, or how to check the facts—

- How do I know this is true?
- Has this happened before?
- Has this happened with other people or in other situations?

Questions about other ways to think about it—

- Is there another way to look at this?
- Is there another reason why this would happen?

Questions about what will happen next—

- Even if this thought is true, what's the worst thing that can happen?
- Even if this thought is true, what's the best thing that can happen?
- What is the most likely thing to happen?

Questions about a plan of attack—

- Is there anything I can do about this?

Call on students to come up with thoughts that would help them feel less worried if they got a D on a math test, using the list of questions as needed. Write down these helpful thoughts in a second column entitled "Helpful Thoughts."

Example negative thought:

- "I'm going to get a bad grade on my report card in math."

Example helpful thoughts:

- "I've done well on other tests."
- "Everyone did badly on this test."
- "I can study more next time."
- "I can ask the teacher if I can earn extra credit to make up for the grade."
- "I can see about getting a tutor."
- "I can ask the teacher for help after school."

Example negative thought:

- "My parents are going to be really mad at me."

Example helpful thoughts:

- "That's not true because they know some tests are really hard."
- "That's not true because they'll understand if I tell them it was really hard."
- "That's not true because they'll understand if I tell them everyone did badly."
- "Even if they are upset, they won't be really mad if I tell them I have a plan to talk to the teacher about raising my grade with extra credit and studying more next time."

Demonstration

*"Now it's time to **practice** coming up with helpful thoughts."*

Introduce the Hot Seat activity, which you will use for the rest of the lesson. Explain that a designated chair is the Hot Seat and that the person who sits in the chair practices coming up with new ways of thinking. Begin by sitting in the Hot Seat yourself. Then, select an example of a negative event.

Example 2

"You are home alone and you hear a noise in the other room."

Select one child to assist you in case you get stuck and can't think of a more realistic approach. Then, instruct the child to provide negative thoughts, one at a time (e.g., "Someone is breaking into the house!" "It's a ghost!"). You will respond by producing alternative thoughts that are more helpful and realistic.

Example helpful thoughts:

- "It could be the wind, the cat, or the house settling."
- "The alarm is set and I didn't hear anything outside the house."
- "It may be my brother or my mom coming home early."

Engagement Activity

Select another example generated from the group. If the group has difficulty generating examples, use one from the list below for the Hot Seat exercise:

> *"Your friend is supposed to call you to arrange a time to pick you up to go out, but he or she hasn't called yet."*

> *"Your parents go out and leave you at home alone."*

> *"You are waiting for the bus, and some older kids start to come down the block."*

Then have the group generate a list of potential negative thoughts.

Next, select a volunteer for the Hot Seat. Select another student as the "coach" to help the child in the Hot Seat challenge negative thoughts. When the child in the Hot Seat gets stuck, have the coach ask one of these questions to help generate helpful realistic counter-thoughts: "Is there another way to look at this? Is there another reason this could happen? What is the worst that could happen? The best that could happen? The most likely thing to happen?" Also be prepared to serve as coach yourself to ensure that the child in the Hot Seat is supported and that strategies for generating helpful thoughts are demonstrated.

Repeat the Hot Seat activity several times with a new situation from students' own examples of recent stressful situations. Use the Hot Seat questions to produce helpful counter-thoughts. Have the group come up with negative thoughts related to the event. Have the child who offered the situation sit in the Hot Seat and dispute the negative thoughts. If the group has difficulty generating scenarios, supply ones that are relevant to the group members and pick anyone in the group to dispute negative thoughts.

Implementation tip

To increase the engagement of all group members, select some children as "recorders" to write positive and negative thoughts on the board as you go, and/or distribute questions to help generate realistic counterthoughts to several groups members so that they may all serve as coaches.

---

4. Plan for Independent Practice

Describe the assignment, which is to practice the Hot Seat thinking at home. Give group members several copies of the worksheets and have them practice with an example before they leave the lesson if there is enough time. Try to give group members specific instructions about the kinds of situations to work on, depending on their needs.

Show group members the "Hot Seat Exercise" worksheet to help them understand how to fill in the worksheet.

5. Review

Briefly review what happened in the group, then preview the next session.

> *"Today we got a lot of practice on ways to challenge negative thinking that is getting in your way. We practiced checking the facts, finding other ways to think about the problem, thinking*

about what will happen next, and making a plan to help solve the problem. We're going to keep practicing the Hot Seat for the rest of the program. Next week, we're going to shift gears a little bit and start talking about facing things you are afraid of. I'm also going to be calling parents this week to check in with them about how things are going and to tell them what we are working on in the support groups."

> **Parent phone call**
>
> Call parents at this point to gain their help and support in the Facing Your Fears assignments that are coming in the next lesson and to remind them of what to expect. Letters will be sent home in Lesson Five if phone calls are not possible.

L4

L4

Lesson Five: Facing Your Fears

1. Introduce Agenda for the Session
2. Independent Practice Review
3. Introduction to Facing Your Fears
4. Picking a Fear to Work On
5. Steps Toward Facing Your Fears
6. Other Coping Strategies to Help Manage Anxiety
7. Plan for Independent Practice
8. Review

Overall Goal

Help students recognize people, places, and/or situations that they may be avoiding in response to their traumatic event. Teach them skills to decrease their anxiety in these situations so that they are able to do everything they once did or want to do.

Student Objectives

1. Students will be able to identify trauma-related avoidance.
2. Students will decrease their anxiety and increase their sense of confidence and mastery by gradually approaching trauma reminders in safe situations.
3. Students will increase their skills for coping with anxiety in these situations.

Materials

1. Copies of the "Steps Toward Facing Your Fears" worksheet (p. 155).
2. Copies of "Facing Your Fears Instructions" (p. 156).
3. Copies of the "Facing Your Fears" and "Hot Seat Exercise" worksheets (pp. 157–159).
4. Copies of the "Letter to Parents" (p. 160), personalized with your signature.
5. "Return to Class" slips (filled out).

Leader Preparation

1. Review students' individual experiences with stress or trauma to assist in identifying possible areas of avoidance. Be prepared to help them identify these areas during group.
2. Review "Helpful Hints for Facing Fears" (p. 154).
3. Personalize the "Letter to Parents" that will be sent home with your signature.

Procedures/Teaching

1.   Introduce Agenda for the Session

Welcome students to the support group and briefly review what will happen in today's lesson.

"Welcome to our fifth group. Today we are going to start by reviewing how things went with your Hot Seat practice during the last week. Then we are going to talk about what happens when we avoid things. Then each of you will pick one thing that you've been avoiding working on and come up with some steps that would allow you to start doing that thing again. I will also teach you some things to help you feel less worried and cope better in these situations. At the end, I will give you another take-home practice for the week that you can bring in during our next meeting."

2.   Independent Practice Review

Review the Hot Seat activities from the previous lesson. Look for the trouble spots listed in Table L5.1 and correct them as indicated.

Table L5.1—How the Leader Can Help Solve Problems with the Hot Seat Activity

Problem	How the Leader Can Help
Didn't do any activities	Attempt to find out why and suggest ways to improve compliance. Ask if the group members noticed any negative thinking during the past week and to describe it. Ask if the students challenged that negative thinking in any way. If so, praise them for work well done. If not, ask them to try to do it right then and to ask for help from other group members if needed.
Couldn't think of any Hot Seat thoughts to challenge negative thinking	Have other group members help the students think of Hot Seat thoughts that could challenge negative thinking. If none are appropriate, remind the group that sometimes negative thinking is realistic and that, in those cases, it's important to try to accept the situation and figure out a way to handle it or solve the problem. (Note that this kind of response is also an "Is there anything I can do?" response.)
The Hot Seat thoughts are unrealistic	Sometimes group members will supply unrealistic Hot Seat thoughts. A few thoughts like this are okay. If this happens too much—to the point where the exercise seems like a joke—ask the group members or the entire group if thinking this way is helpful. Remind them that they are trying to correct thinking that is unhelpful or untrue (go back to the Chicken Little example), not come up with more unhelpful thinking.

3.   Introduction to Facing Your Fears

The goal of this part of the lesson is to introduce the idea that avoidance is one form of coping with anxiety-provoking events, but that it usually creates more problems than it solves. Begin with an example (from the group, if possible) of an anxiety-provoking event.

"Let's take an example. What kinds of things make you really nervous or afraid? [Possible examples are the first day at school, a big test at school, asking someone out for a date, performing something in front of an audience, going somewhere new alone.]

"Have you ever felt so nervous about something that you wished you could get away with skipping it altogether? Did you ever try to do that—avoid doing something? This is a common way to handle stress: Try to avoid it. But what happens when you avoid something? Does the problem go away? Do you ever miss out on things you want to happen because you avoid something? [Discuss their experiences.]

"There's another problem with avoiding things. The more you avoid something, the scarier that thing seems. [Use a relevant example here, or use the one that follows.]

"Let's say you are really nervous about starting in a new school. You wish you didn't have to go there at all. You feel sick; you are all tense.

"If you stayed home the first day, how do you think you'd feel the second day? Would you feel less nervous, the same, or more nervous? [Make the point that they'd probably feel even more nervous: Since they'd be one day behind, others would know each other, etc.]

"What if you went ahead and went to school on that first day, even though you were nervous? How would you feel the second day? [Make the point that they would probably feel less nervous as each day went on, as long as nothing bad happened.]"

Use other examples, as necessary, until the group members are convinced that repeated exposure to feared events will make them less afraid. Possible examples include performances (sports, dance, music), speaking in class, going to unfamiliar places, and trying new things.

"In this group, we're going to start to work on things that make us nervous or upset, and we're going to do them again and again until we feel okay and are able to do all the things we used to do or want to do."

4.   Picking a Fear to Work On

The goal of this part of the lesson is to have each student pick something that he or she has been avoiding or has stopped doing since the trauma happened. As the group leader, you may already know about things like this for certain group members, either from the discussion in Lesson Two or from examples they have given. If so, you can help steer them toward those fears during this exercise. For others, you will need to help them find something to work on during this section. Priority should be given to a situation that is trauma-related. If nothing trauma-related can be found, you can replace it with another feared situation, like giving a speech in front of others. Group members will need help along the way, since stress or trauma survivors are often unaware of these types of situations (especially if they are avoiding them effectively).

There are several important things to discuss with group members as they choose the situation they want to work on:

1.   The situation needs to be **safe**. List only things that the children should feel comfortable doing. Examples of situations that would not work are

- being exposed to violence in person
- doing anything dangerous (e.g., climbing onto something high up)
- being in an unsafe environment (e.g., out alone in a deserted area at night).

If group members list such things, tell them that those things are supposed to make people nervous because they are dangerous. You are trying to help them feel less nervous in situations in which they are supposed to feel okay. Tell them that in a few minutes you will introduce ways to calm down when these things happen.

There are a few questions you can ask the children if you are not sure if a situation is safe or dangerous, and their answers should help you figure out whether to recommend that they work on the situation:

- Are other people like you (your age, gender, ethnicity) there at that time or doing the same thing?
- What do your parents think? Do they think this is safe for you?
- What do your friends think?
- Would your friends do that? If they have done it, have they been safe?

2. Some situations are designed to make people feel nervous or excited and are therefore hard to work on. These include watching scary movies and riding roller coasters. Explain to the children that part of the fun of these things is to feel scared, and make sure that they really want to work on these things.

3. The lists should include things that the children are avoiding, but the children may not be sure how anxious they would be in these situations. Ask them to guess how nervous or upset the thing or situation would make them.

"To start, I want each of you to pick something that is making you afraid because of the stress or trauma that happened to you. I'll ask some questions to help you think about what you might want to work on:

- *Is there anything that you used to enjoy but stopped doing because of the stress or trauma? This might be things like hanging out with your friends in certain places or activities that involve being alone or out at night.*
- *Are there any things that you used to do regularly that you stopped doing after the stress or trauma you went through? For example, going to places that remind you of what happened, doing things like you were doing when the stress or trauma happened?*
- *Have you started avoiding things like being alone in certain places, being in the dark, or sleeping by yourself?*
- *Do you avoid talking to people about what happened? Is there anyone that you'd like to be able to talk to about it?*
- *Do you avoid reading things or watching certain TV programs that would remind you about what happened?*
- *Do you avoid certain objects or people that would make you nervous or upset because they were there when it happened?*

"Who can tell me a situation like that they would like to work on being able to do again?"

If no one volunteers, you can choose a student for whom you know a situation to work on, remind them of it, and use it to work on. Go around the room and figure out one problem for each student that is "workable," meaning a situation that

- is getting in the student's way somehow, and that he or she wants to fix
- is relatively safe (e.g., is something other students do in the child's neighborhood)
- is not a scary movie, roller coaster, or something else that is supposed to make people anxious, but rather something that most people do without anxiety
- can probably be broken into some steps, as seen in the following section.

Examples of good exercises include the following, with parental supervision in place: crossing roads at traffic lights, sleeping with the lights off or with the door closed, looking at pictures that remind them of the trauma, visiting a location that is similar to one in which the trauma occurred (if it is safe, such as a shopping mall, school, park, market, or other public place).

5. Steps Toward Facing Your Fears

The goal of this part of the lesson is to break the situation chosen by each student into steps. Use the "Steps Toward Facing Your Fears" worksheet and the "Facing Your Fears Instructions" to guide this process.

Engagement Activity

Give students the handouts, having them first focus on the "Steps Toward Facing Your Fears" worksheet. Ask them to write their situation on the top of their worksheet in the slot labeled "10."

> *"Begin by writing in the situation you just picked at the top of the stairs, where it has a '10.' We put it there because it's hard for you to do and would make you feel very anxious or upset if you did it right now. It may not be a '10' for you, so you can cross that out and put a different number if you want, but it should be a high number if we are going to work on it. Now, our job is to break it down into easier steps, to find something that would be less upsetting or would make you less nervous."*

Draw the steps up on the board and use an example to guide them through this process. For instance, you could put the situation "Going to the park where I saw the shooting, alone, around dinnertime."

> *"Let's start with the step that says '2.' Here you need to think of something that is much easier to do and would only make you feel about a '2' on the Fear Thermometer. For instance, what if you just imagine doing it, but don't really do it? Would that be a '2' for you? Or if you looked pictures of the situation instead of doing it? Or drew a picture of it? Would any of those be a '2' for you?"*

Go around the room and help students find a very easy way of approaching each situation, such as using imagination or looking at pictures. Write on your example, on the '2' step, "Thinking about going to the park in my imagination."

"Does everyone have something to write there? Okay, let me ask a few questions to make sure it's a good one:

- *Would you be safe if you tried that?*
- *Is this something you could do this week?*
- *Will this help you work toward your '10' situation?"*

Show them that the situation you wrote in the example is safe, something you can do this week, and will help you work toward your goal. If students answer "no" to any of these questions, help them adjust their steps so that the answer becomes "yes."

"Now let's move on to the middle steps, labeled '4' and '6' and '8' on the Fear Thermometer. We need to figure out some steps in the middle that will get you from your '2' situation to being able to try your '10' situation. For instance, if your '10' is something you want to be able to do alone, your '4' or '6' step might be doing that same thing with other people. Or if you want to be able to do something at night, you could try it during the daytime first—that might be a good '8' step. For my example, I think that going to the park in the morning, before people start to hang out there, would be an '8' if I did it alone and a '4' if I did it with my mother. If I went there around dinnertime with my mother, it would be a good '6.' I'm going to write those in on the steps."

Write the examples on the middle steps and show the students that you are asking questions about whether each step is safe, can be done this week, etc. Then go around the room and ask students to tell you situations that fall in the middle steps. Have the students write the steps on the worksheet.

6. Other Coping Strategies to Help Manage Anxiety

Begin by asking the group what they can do if they feel anxious or nervous when they are in some way reminded of the trauma (such as by the things or situations on their lists). Discuss how they can use skills they've already learned about in the group to help with this. Remind group members of the relaxation exercise taught in Lesson Two and review or practice the exercise as a group if necessary. Also, remind group members that challenging negative thoughts and generating helpful thoughts can help them manage their anxiety and have more success in facing these situations.

After some group discussion, practice the following techniques:

- **Thought stopping.** Begin by asking the group to think about the traumas that they experienced. Ask them to think about what happened; what it looked like; what they heard, saw, smelled, tasted, thought about, and felt. Facilitate this imaginative process for a minute or so, and then say, "STOP!" loudly to distract the group. Ask them what they are thinking about now. Most will tell you that they are thinking about you, or the other group members, or about nothing at all. Explain that this is the thought stopping technique. Another way that kids can use this technique is by suddenly imagining a big red stop sign in their mind that interrupts their thoughts. Encourage them to talk about ways they can use this technique when upsetting thoughts are bothering them.

L5

- **Distraction.** Next discuss distraction. Ask for examples from the group members about how they distract themselves when they are upset. These can include playing video games, listening to music, calling or talking to a friend, getting involved in a book or TV program, exercising, or playing sports.
- **Positive imagery.** Another way to reduce anxiety is to change negative images into positive ones, or to replace negative thoughts and images with positive ones. Have group members tell you things that they love to do or really great things that happened to them. Examples include playing basketball, lying on the beach, taking a warm bath, going to a concert, hiking in the mountains, riding a bike, or some particularly meaningful event. Ask group members to close their eyes and imagine this scene or event, helping them build the image by asking such questions as "How do you feel? What are you doing? What is going on around you? What do you hear? What do you smell or taste?"

Explain that if they practice a technique enough, they will be able to call it up in times of stress to reduce anxiety. The have each group member pick one or two techniques to practice.

7.   Plan for Independent Practice

Refer students to "Facing Your Fears Instructions" and the "Facing Your Fears" take-home activity worksheet. Read through "Facing Your Fears Instructions" to ensure that students have a good idea about what they will be practicing while ensuring safety and effective duration. This time, students will work on the first two steps, the "2" step and the "4" step. Have them write these steps on the lines below the phrase "This week, I am going to" on their "Facing Your Fears" worksheet.

After they write down the two things, ask them to talk to you about when and where they are going to do them. Have them write this information in the boxes on their worksheets. Ask them how they will explain the activity to their parents. Be sure to assess the safety of the situations and help the children make adjustments as necessary to ensure they are supported by parents and will be safe during the activity. Show the children how to mark the "Fear Thermometer Rating" boxes with the levels from their Fear Thermometers before and after the activity and also to note the highest Fear Thermometer level they experienced. Show the children how to fill in the boxes each time they do the activity.

Give the students copies of the "Hot Seat Exercise" worksheet to continue practicing at home.

Alert the students to another "Letter to Parents" and ask them to have it filled out and signed. Remind them to bring it to the next meeting along with the rest of their materials.

8.   Review

Briefly review what happened in the group, then preview the next session.

"Today we talked about things we avoid because they make us feel anxious. We talked about how we can approach them to 'face our fears.' We also talked about relaxation and other ways to cope with anxiety or nervousness. Next time, we'll start writing about the traumatic or stressful things that happened to each of us."

Lesson Six: Trauma Narrative, Part One

> 1. Introduce Agenda for the Session
> 2. Independent Practice Review
> 3. Writing a Newspaper Story About the Trauma
> 4. Plan for Independent Practice
> 5. Review

Overall Goal

Help students begin to process their traumatic experience through writing about it and sharing their story with the rest of the group.

Student Objectives

1. Students will understand why it is important to write about and share their traumas.
2. Student will write a newspaper-style story about their traumatic events.
3. Students will read their stories to the rest of the group.
4. Students will support one another during the sharing process.
5. Students will feel less anxiety when they think about the trauma.

Materials

1. Copies of the "Writing a Newspaper Story" worksheet (pp. 162–163).
2. Copies of the "A Newspaper Picture" worksheet (p. 164).
3. Copies of the "Facing Your Fears" and "Hot Seat Exercise" worksheets (pp. 165–167).
4. "Return to Class" slips (filled out).

Leader Preparation

1. Review each student's traumatic event.
2. Review Table 4, Common Misconceptions About Processing Trauma (p. 26).

Procedures/Teaching

1. Introduce Agenda for the Session

Welcome students to the support group and briefly review what will happen in today's lesson.

L6

"Today we are going to start working on processing the traumatic events that happened to all of you. We'll begin by reviewing the assignments from last time, and then you will each work by yourself for a while to write out the story of what happened to you as if you were writing it for a newspaper. Then we'll have time for each one of you to share your story with the group. At the end, we'll do a review and I'll give out some new assignments."

2.   Independent Practice Review

Review the children's progress with the Facing Your Fears homework. Highlight the fact that, if practiced enough, anxiety or upset will decrease. Give a few examples of this in the group. Look for the problems listed in Table L6.1 and discuss potential solutions.

Table L6.1—How the Leader Can Help Solve Problems with the Facing Your Fears Activity

Problem	How the Leader Can Help
Didn't do the activities	Explore why and look for avoidance. Use this opportunity to review negative thoughts and practice Hot Seat exercises if possible. For example, ask, "When it was time to do the activity, what thought popped into your head that made you decide not to do it?"
Started to do it, but felt upset and cut it short	Commend the student for his or her courage, but point out that this won't help him or her feel better. Reiterate the assignment and the need to stick with it until anxiety decreases. Talk about ways to redo the assignment in the coming week with more support or using an easier fear.
Logistics interfered	Problem solve with the group to figure out ways to get around barriers to the assignment.
Did it but never felt upset	This could mean that the group member is making progress or somehow avoiding the assignment (e.g., using some kind of "security blanket" or safety net that makes the situation somehow not count). Examples of this include having someone there for support or doing it at a certain time of day. Explore whether there was anything special that made the student feel okay. If so, consider asking him or her to remove that part of the experience to make the assignment more challenging next time. Remember that the goal is to eliminate all stress- or trauma-related avoidance. Unless the group member is likely to encounter a particular situation in his or her real life, it is not necessary to work on it.
Started to feel unsafe because something happened	If something happened that was potentially dangerous (or that would cause anxiety in anyone who was there), this reaction is normal and healthy. Congratulate group members on their good judgment in detecting real danger. Discuss ways to plan the next assignment to avoid any real danger and involve the group in solving this problem. Remind group members that you are working on stress- or trauma-related distress, not trying to make sure they never feel upset again.
Said they did the homework, but it is not really believable	Ask for details in order to get a better idea of whether they did it or not. Do not confront them about it if you think they are lying to you, but do make sure to plan the next activity carefully with them and make sure it is something they can realistically accomplish.

L6

As you review successes, note other fears from the "Steps Toward Facing Your Fears" worksheet that would be appropriate for each group member so that the activity at the end of Lesson Six is easier.

3.   Writing Newspaper Story About the Trauma

Begin the lesson by explaining the rationale for writing a trauma narrative. Answer any questions that the students have. The following example can be used:

"Have you ever eaten too much all at once and felt really full and sick afterwards? And you wish you hadn't eaten that much? Your stomach feels sick because it's got too much in it at once. That food feels like it's filling up your whole body. Your stomach has more than it can handle.

"The way you think about the stressful event you went through can also feel like that— it's too much to digest at once, so it bothers you a lot. Just like with the meal, you need to "digest" it sooner or later. Even though the stress probably seems really overwhelming when you think about it now, eventually, with enough work, we can make it smaller.

"Today we're going to help you start to digest it by writing about it. We'll also make a plan for how to continue digesting it for the rest of the group lessons.

"By thinking about the stress or trauma where it is safe (here with me or in the group), a couple of things will happen:

- *Over time, if you work on digesting the stress or trauma, you will feel less upset each time you think about it. By the end of group, you will be able to think about what happened and feel okay.*
- *You will learn that thinking about the stress or trauma won't make you flip out or go crazy, that it's just a bad memory that can't hurt you anymore.*
- *You will learn that you can take control of the way you feel and do something to make yourself feel better."*

Engagement Activity

The goal of this part of the lesson is to write the trauma narrative in a journalistic style, focused mostly on facts. (In the next lesson, students will write about the trauma from the first-person perspective and include more details and emotions in their story.) Introduce the activity by passing out the "Writing a Newspaper Story" worksheet. Explain to students that at the top of the worksheet, they should fill in the facts of what happened in their traumatic experience:

- Who was there?
- What happened?
- When did it happen?
- Where did it happen?
- Why did it happen?
- How did it happen?

After they fill in this information, they will convert it into a two-paragraph newspaper story by writing sentences that contain that information. Let group members know ahead of time that you do not want them to provide too much detail to the other group members about what happened because it's hard for others to hear so many stories. Remind them that newspaper articles usually do not have room to include too many details. Circulate around the room to make sure that students are on task and not having too much trouble.

Engagement Activity

After they write their stories, tell group members that you want them to share their stories with the rest of the group. Begin by reminding them about confidentiality and the contract they signed at the beginning of group. Explain that this is a time when they will need to be extra careful not to talk about things that happened to other people.

Next, discuss what feels supportive and unsupportive in situations like these, and have students identify the kind of support that they want from the group. Pick a student that you think will provide a good example to go first. Follow the steps below for each group member.

"One thing that is really important for people when they share something like this is for them to feel supported by other people.

"Let's talk for a minute about what we mean by 'support.' Pretend that you share something really personal with a group of people. If someone leans over and whispers to someone else while you are talking, is that supportive? Why or why not? If someone makes eye contact with you and smiles or nods at you while you are talking, is that supportive? Why or why not? If people laugh during or after you talk, is that supportive? Why or why not?

"Generally, paying attention to someone and showing respect is a good way to be supportive."

First, ask the student you've chosen what kind of support he or she would like from the group.

"What kind of support or feedback would you like to get from the other group members when you tell them about what happened to you? Is there a particular person in the group that you want to get support or feedback from? Is there anything you want others to be careful not to say or do after you share?"

Ask the student to read his or her story out loud to the group. Then ask other group members to offer the kind of support that was requested. Be careful to make sure that the other group members do not make judgmental comments or ignore the disclosure. If any of this does occur, process it by reviewing common reactions to stress or trauma and normalizing other group members' reactions. Model offering supportive statements yourself first, then ask group members to say something as well. Do not allow group members to ignore or make fun of each other.

4.   Plan for Independent Practice

Hand out the "A Newspaper Picture" worksheet. Ask students to draw a picture to accompany their newspaper story. They can draw what they would want a photograph that would go with the story to look like if it were in a real newspaper.

Hand out the Facing Your Fears assignments using the "Facing Your Fears" worksheet. Fill in relevant examples with students if possible.

L6

Hand out the "Hot Seat Exercise" worksheet, filling in relevant examples if possible. Ask the students to fill out this worksheet and the others, and to bring them to the next lesson.

5.   Review

Briefly review what happened in the group, then preview the next session.

"Today you all did great work in writing about what happened to you. This exercise should help you feel a little bit better over time because you are facing your fears and are processing what happened to you. Next time, we'll do some more writing like this, but we'll write a different kind of story about the same thing."

Lesson Seven: Trauma Narrative, Part Two

1. Introduce Agenda for the Session	4. Plan for Independent Practice
2. Independent Practice Review	5. Review
3. Writing a Personal Trauma Story	

Overall Goal

Help students begin to process their traumatic experience through writing about it and sharing their stories with the rest of the group.

Student Objectives

1. Students will understand why it is important to write about and share their traumas.
2. Students will write a personal story about their traumatic events.
3. Students will read their stories to the rest of the group.
4. Students will support one another during the sharing process.
5. Students will feel less anxiety when they think about the trauma.

Materials

1. Copies of the "Personal Story" worksheet (pp. 170–171).
2. Copies of the "Personal Story Picture" worksheet (p. 172).
3. Copies of the "Facing Your Fears" and "Hot Seat Exercise" worksheets (pp. 173–175).
4. "Return to Class" slips (filled out).

L7

Leader Preparation

1. Review each student's traumatic event.
2. Review Table 4, Common Misconceptions About Processing Trauma (p. 26).

Procedures/Teaching

1. Introduce Agenda for the Session

Welcome students to the support group and briefly review what will happen in today's lesson.

"Today we are going to continue our work from the last lesson. We'll keep on working on pro-cessing the traumatic events that happened to all of you. We'll begin by reviewing the assign-ments from last time, and then you will each work by yourself for a while to write out the story of what happened to you. This time it will be a more personal story. Like last time, we'll have time for each one of you to share your story with the group. At the end, we'll do a review and I'll give out some new assignments."

2. Independent Practice Review

Review the activities with group members, asking how they felt when they drew the pictures about the stresses or traumas. Look for the trouble spots Listed in Table L7.1 and correct them as indicated. (Be sure to review the other assignments as well, checking in on Facing Your Fears and Hot Seat practice.)

Table L7.1—How the Leader Can Help Solve Problems with the Newspaper Picture Activity

Problem	How the Leader Can Help
Didn't do any activities	Explore reasons for this. Was it fear? Reluctance to feel upset? Wanting to avoid thinking about the stress or trauma? If so, review the rationale for the support group. If possible, engage other group members to help you convince the child that this work is valuable, though painful. Try to come up with a relevant analogy (e.g., "no pain, no gain") that will motivate the child. Remind him or her that this work is time-limited: He or she will not need to do it again once the group is over. Use this opportunity to review negative thoughts and practice Hot Seat exercises if possible. For example, ask, "When it was time to do the activities, what thoughts popped into your head that made you decide not to do them?"
Didn't have time/privacy/etc.	Work on logistical barriers to activity completion with group members to ensure success in the coming week. Gently explore other possible reasons for reluctance, as listed immediately above.
Didn't bother me/wasn't upsetting	This could either mean progress or avoidance. Explore whether the group member did the exercise fully and was working on the painful parts of the memory. If it seems that he or she did it correctly, it is possible that the memory just isn't as painful as expected. If the exercise wasn't done correctly, gently confront avoidance and make it a point to work on those areas in the rest of the lesson.
Felt awful/too upsetting	Reframe this as positive and courageous work on the problem. Remind the group member that it takes time before the memory becomes less upsetting, but that he or she is doing what needs to be done in order to feel better. Closely monitor exposure in the rest of the lesson and help the group member modulate emotions (e.g., slow down with relaxation) during the exercise so that he or she can do this at home as well.

L7

3.   Writing a Personal Trauma Story

Begin the lesson by reminding students about the rationale for writing a trauma narrative. Answer any questions that the students have. The following script can be used:

> *"Last week you began the important job of processing or digesting what happened to you. This week, we want to go even a little bit further with that. This time, I am going to ask you to write a story about what happened **from your perspective, including your thoughts and feelings when it happened.** That includes what happened around you, but also what happened to you, how your body reacted, or what you thought or heard or saw. So, it will be more about you and what you experienced. As I described last week, writing it down and sharing it will help you digest the entire experience."*

Engagement Activity

The goal of this part of the lesson is to write the trauma narrative from a first-person perspective, with the students themselves being the main characters. Unlike the newspaper style in the last lesson, this story will include the students' thoughts, feelings, sensations, and actions. Introduce the activity by passing out the "Personal Story" worksheet. Explain to students that at the top of the worksheet are some questions to help plan their stories. After they answer those questions, they can use their answers to form their personal stories. The questions are listed here:

- When will your story begin?
- When will your story end?
- Make a list below of the things you will want to include in your story:
  - key things that happened
  - feelings or emotions that you had
  - thoughts you had
  - sensations or feelings in your body that you had.
- What is the most important point that you want to make about what happened to you?
- What do you want make sure that other people understand about what happened to you?

After they fill in this information, they will convert it into a three- or four-paragraph story by writing sentences that contain the information. Circulate around the room to make sure that students are on task and not having too much trouble.

Engagement Activity

After they write their stories, tell group members that you want them to share their stories with the rest of the group.

Begin by reminding them again about confidentiality. Then pick a student who you think will provide a good example to go first. Follow these steps for each group member:

First, ask the student you've chosen what kind of support he or she would like from the group.

> *"What kind of support or feedback would you like to get from the other group members when you tell them about what happened to you? Is there a particular person in the group that you*

L7

want to get support or feedback from? Is there anything you want others to be careful not to say or do after you share?"

Ask the student to read his or her story out loud to the group. Then ask other group members to offer the kind of support that was requested. Be careful to make sure that the other group members do not make judgmental comments or ignore the disclosure. If any of this does occur, process it by reviewing common reactions to stress or trauma and normalizing other group members' reactions. Model offering supportive statements yourself first, then ask group members to say something as well. Do not allow group members to ignore or make fun of each other.

4.   Plan for Independent Practice

Hand out the "Personal Story Picture" worksheet. Ask students to draw a picture to accompany their personal story. They can draw a picture to go along with any part of the story that they choose. Ask the group members to spend time looking at their pictures or reading their stories. If they feel comfortable, they could also read their stories to a family member or close friend.

Ask the students to continue the Facing Your Fears assignments using the "Facing Your Fears" worksheet.

Ask the students to practice the Hot Seat exercise using the "Hot Seat Exercise" worksheet. Ask the students to fill out this worksheet and the others, and to bring them to the next lesson.

5.   Review

Briefly review what happened in the group, then preview the next session.

"Today you wrote more-personal stories about your traumatic or stressful experiences, and that will help you even more. I hope you are all feeling a little more comfortable when you think about what happened to you. Next time, we're going to start working on solving some of the problems in your lives, like problems with friends or family members."

L7

L7

Lesson Eight: Problem Solving

1.	Introduce Agenda for the Session	4.	Brainstorming Solutions
2.	Independent Practice Review	5.	Decision Making: Pros and Cons
3.	Introduction to Social Problem Solving	6.	Plan for Independent Practice
		7.	Review

Overall Goal

Teach students skills required to solve real-life problems.

Student Objectives

1. Students will learn about the link between thoughts and actions.
2. Students will learn to brainstorm solutions to a problem.
3. Students will learn to evaluate the pros and cons of various solutions to problems.
4. Students will begin to apply skills to problems in their own lives.

Materials

1. Copies of the "Problem Solving" worksheet (p. 178).
2. Copies of the "Facing Your Fears" and "Hot Seat Exercise" worksheets (pp. 179–181).
3. "Return to Class" slips (filled out).

Leader Preparation

1. Compile a list of real-life problems faced by students in the current group. Prepare to use these as examples in the lesson.

L8

Procedures/Teaching

1. Introduce Agenda for the Session

Welcome students to the support group and briefly review what will happen in today's lesson.

"Today we are going to start working on ways to help with some of the problems that you are all having in your lives, ones not necessarily related to the trauma that happened to you. We'll begin by reviewing the assignments from last time, then we'll start talking about the way that

thoughts and actions are linked. We'll do a brainstorming exercise for a real-life problem, and then we'll talk about how to decide what to do about problems. At the end, we'll do a review, and I'll give out some new assignments."

2.   Independent Practice Review

Review the activities with group members, as you did in the last lesson. Ask how they felt when drawing about the stress or trauma. Look for the trouble spots listed in Table L8.1 and correct them as indicated. (Be sure to review the other assignments as well, checking in on Facing Your Fears and Hot Seat practice.)

Table L8.1—How the Leader Can Help Solve Problems with the Personal Story Picture Activity

Problem	How the Leader Can Help
Didn't do any activities	Explore reasons for this. Was it fear? Reluctance to feel upset? Wanting to avoid thinking about the stress or trauma? If so, review the rationale for the support group. If possible, engage other group members to help you convince the child that this work is valuable, though painful. Try to come up with a relevant analogy (e.g., "no pain, no gain") that will motivate the child. Remind him or her that this work is time-limited: He or she will not need to do it again once the group is over. Use this opportunity to review negative thoughts and practice Hot Seat exercises if possible. For example, ask, "When it was time to do the activities, what thoughts popped into your head that made you decide not to do them?"
Didn't have time/privacy/etc.	Work on logistical barriers to activity completion with group members to ensure success in the coming week. Gently explore other possible reasons for reluctance, as listed immediately above.
Didn't bother me/wasn't upsetting	This could either mean progress or avoidance. Explore whether the group member did the exercise fully and was working on the painful parts of the memory. If it seems that he or she did it correctly, it is possible that the memory just isn't as painful as expected. If the exercise wasn't done correctly, gently confront avoidance and make it a point to work on those areas in the rest of the lesson.
Felt awful/too upsetting	Reframe this as positive and courageous work on the problem. Remind the group member that it takes time before the memory becomes less upsetting, but that he or she is doing what needs to be done in order to feel better. Closely monitor exposure in the rest of the lesson and help the group member modulate emotions (e.g., slow down with relaxation) during the exercise so that he or she can do this at home as well.

L8

3. Introduction to Social Problem Solving[1]

The purpose of this part of the lesson is to briefly introduce the idea that solving problems with other people takes practice. Begin by asking group members to list conflicts or problems they have with friends or family members; write these on the board. Add to the list any problems you have noticed during the earlier lessons. As much as possible, draw from this list of problems during the rest of the lesson. In choosing examples for the group, consider the types of symptoms the students are expressing and how well the students work together in the group. Two types of examples are possible: (1) a general example drawing on common peer or family problems (but about anxiety and/or avoidance) and (2) a stress- or trauma-focused example relating to social situations (e.g., disclosure about abuse, avoidance that interferes with friendships). Both examples are shown in this section. Introduce social problem solving as follows:

"Sometimes people think they are upset because they have 'real problems' and 'anyone who had these problems would be upset.'

*"If you feel this way, you usually think you have to solve the problem in order to feel better. But that's not true. You **do** have some control over feeling better.*

"There are four parts to every problem:

- *physical (objective, measurable) events*
- *how others think and act*
- *how you think*
- *how you act or what you do.*

"We can work today on how you think about things and how you act on them."

Engagement Activity

In this activity, students learn the ways in which thoughts influence behavior with friends and family members. Students should learn that thoughts lead to different actions and that one way to change the way we act with friends and family is to check our thinking about what happened. Begin by reading one of the following examples to the group.

Example 1 (General)

"Tom's friends are all going to a dance at school, and all of them have asked dates. Tom is the only one who hasn't asked anyone yet. Tom is afraid that the person he likes, Yolanda, won't want to go with him, so he's been avoiding asking her. He is walking down the hall and sees Yolanda talking to a guy in his class, and he thinks, 'She's going to the dance with him.' So he turns the corner to avoid her and goes straight home from school."

Make two headings for columns on the board: "Thoughts" and "Actions."

---

[1] This introduction about the "healthy management of reality" is derived from Muñoz, R. F., & Miranda, J. (1986). Group Therapy Manual for Cognitive-Behavioral Treatment of Depression. San Francisco General Hospital, Depression Clinic. (Activities—Lesson 4), and, as modified for adolescents, in Asarnow, J., Jaycox, L. H., Clarke, G., Lewinsohn, P., Hops, H., & Rohde, P. (1999). Stress and Your Mood: A Manual. Los Angeles: UCLA School of Medicine.

L8

"In this example, what did Tom think? What did he do?"

Write thoughts and actions in two columns on the board as in the example table below.

Thoughts	Actions
She's going to the dance with him.	Do **not** ask her out—go home.
She's telling him that she likes **me**.	Go up now and ask her out.
They are talking about school.	Find her later and ask her out.
Maybe she's going to the dance with him.	Ask around and see if that's true.
If she says no, I can ask someone else.	Ask her first, then someone else.

"You can see that what Tom did made complete sense, given what he thought. Who can tell me some other ways to think about this problem?"

List several other thoughts, as in the example table. Then review each thought and say what Tom would do if he was thinking that way.

Example 2 (Trauma-Related)

"You tell one friend about what happened to you, and she doesn't say much to you and leaves a little while later. You go to school the next day, and your friend is talking with a group of other kids. You think your friend is telling them what happened to you, and you feel really mad and upset. You avoid her and hang up on her when she calls you at home that night.

"In this example, what did you think? What did you do?"

As before, write thoughts and actions in two columns on the board as in the example table below.

Thoughts	Actions
She told everyone what happened to me.	Avoid everyone.
They all feel sorry for me.	Get some sympathy from them.
They all think I'm a reject.	Avoid everyone.
She's busy with them now, but she wouldn't tell them about me.	Catch up with her later.
It's going to take her some time to realize what I went through. Then she'll be nice to me again.	Let it go for now, but talk to her when she calls.
She's not a good friend after all.	Realize she isn't trustworthy, but try to talk to someone else about it another time.

L8

"You can see that what you did made complete sense, given what you thought. Who can tell me some other ways to think about this problem?"

List several other thoughts. Then review each thought and say what you would do if you were thinking this way.

To summarize, make the following point:

"These examples show us that different thoughts about a problem will lead to doing things differently to handle the problem. So, it is important to make sure that your thinking is accurate before you decide what to do. Sometimes you'll need to use the Hot Seat in order to make sure your thinking is accurate before you act."

4.   Brainstorming Solutions

The goal of this part of the lesson is to practice generating lots of solutions to real-life problems so that group members aren't "locked in" to one type of response (often based on faulty thinking). This part of the lesson is especially important for those group members who tend to act impulsively. It helps them slow down the thought process and give themselves more options for how to act. Encourage group members to be creative but also to include appropriate behaviors as much as possible. Two types of solutions that are almost always possible are

- seeking social support
- trying to get more information about a problem.

Follow through with the examples used in the previous section, or use a new example based on issues that have come up.

Example 1 (General)

"What are some different things that Tom could do in this situation? Let's list them on the board."

Add these additional options to the list on the board:

- Ask her if she's going to the dance, and if not, ask her out.
- Ask her friends if she's going to the dance.
- If she's going to the dance, think of someone else to ask.
- Decide not to go to the dance, but make some other plans.

Example 2 (Trauma-Related)

"What are some different things that you could do in this situation? Let's list them on the board."

Add these additional options to the list on the board:

- Ask your friend if she told others.
- If she did tell others, explain to her how you feel about it.

L8

- Try to find friends who are more trustworthy.
- Shake it off—it doesn't matter if they know what happened.

Engagement Activity

Divide the group into two teams. Write a problem on the board and ask each team to come up with as many different solutions (things someone could do to try to improve the situation) as possible. Tell them that the team that comes up with the most possible actions will win the competition. Then reconvene as a group and review all the possibilities generated. If students offer highly negative, aggressive, or inappropriate answers, shape them into more-neutral answers when you reflect them back, but accept them as valid answers. Try to probe for a variety of different types of answers, then move directly into the next section on pros and cons. Examples of responses to inappropriate answers are listed in Table L8.2.

Table L8.2—Suggested Leader Responses to Inappropriate Answers

Student Answer	Your Response
"Shoot him! Kill him!"	*"Okay, so you could be aggressive, try to hurt him. Let's add that to the list. How well would that work for you? What are the pros and cons for that one?"* (See below.)
"Get your friends to beat him up."	*"Okay, another thing you could do to hurt him. But this time, get your friends to help. We'll add that, but again, let's think about the pros and cons."* (See below.)
"You could plant drugs in his locker and then tip off security."	*"Another thing to get him in trouble or get him hurt. We've got three of those kinds of ideas now. Can anyone think of anything a little bit different? Is there another type of response that might help with the problem?"*

5.   Decision Making: Pros and Cons

The goal of this part of the lesson is to evaluate the possible actions the children are considering. For younger groups, use the terminology "pluses and minuses"; for older groups, use "pros and cons." Pick one of the favorite actions that goes with the two examples given above in Section 3, Introduction to Social Problem Solving, and write it on the board. Then make two columns: "Pluses" (or "Pros") and "Minuses" (or "Cons").

Engagement Activity

Divide the group into two teams and ask them to generate reasons why the favorite action would be a good or bad thing to do. Encourage them to come up with items in both columns. Review their answers as a group. Make sure that students are "fair" in considering **both** pros and cons.

6.   Plan for Independent Practice

The activities for this lesson involve picking a current interpersonal problem and using the worksheets to problem solve. Spend a few minutes with group members individually, selecting interpersonal problems. If they can't think of problems, select ones that they have worked on

L8

in earlier lessons. Also select additional topics from the "Facing Your Fears" activity in Lesson Five for real-life exposure. Be sure to work with each group member to work out the details of the assignment.

Ask the students to complete the "Problem Solving Practice" worksheet.

Ask the students to continue the Facing Your Fears assignments using the "Facing Your Fears" worksheet.

Ask the students to practice the Hot Seat exercise using the "Hot Seat Exercise" worksheet. Ask the students to fill out this worksheet and the others, and to bring them to the next lesson.

7.   Review

Briefly review what happened in the group, then preview the next session.

"Today we worked on how to solve problems in your life, such as problems with family members and friends. The next time we meet, we're going to practice that some more, and we're also going to practice the Hot Seat exercise."

Lesson Nine: Practice with Social Problems and the Hot Seat

1. Introduce Agenda for the Session	4. Review of Key Concepts
2. Independent Practice Review	5. Plan for Independent Practice
3. Practice with Problem Solving and the Hot Seat	6. Review

Overall Goal

Increase students' competence in challenging negative thoughts and handling real-life problems.

Student Objectives

1. Students will build additional competencies and fluency in challenging negative thinking through practice.
2. Students will build additional competencies and fluency in solving real-life and interpersonal problems.
3. Students will take steps toward solving some problems in their own lives via a combination of these two skills.

Materials

1. Copies of the "Evaluation Form" (pp. 184–185).
2. "Return to Class" slips (filled out).

Leader Preparation

1. Consider each student's continuing problems and symptoms and plan to address them in the remaining two sessions.
2. Consult with supervisor on the need to refer any students into counseling or therapy after the group ends.

Procedures/Teaching

1. Introduce Agenda for the Session

Welcome students to the support group and briefly review what will happen in today's lesson.

L9

"Today we are going to keep practicing solving problems and challenging negative thoughts. We'll tackle some more of the problems you are having in your lives. Next time will be our last meeting, so I'm not going to give you anything to practice between this group and the next one. Since this time and next are our last opportunities to help one another in the group, make sure you bring up the problems you want help with."

2. Independent Practice Review

Review the problem-solving assignment. Review obstacles to problem-solving practice and ask the group to generate new ideas for how to handle it if a group member is stuck. Note that some group members will not be able to overcome problems because of the nature of those problems. When this happens, point out that the group members made their best efforts, but not everything is under their control. Point out that they **can** control how they think and act, and, therefore, how they feel about the problem. Also remind them that they can always seek social support or try to find out more about a problem. Help group members find ways to feel better about the situations, using Hot Seat exercises or suggesting relaxation, if appropriate. Some examples are provided in Table L9.1.

Table L9.1—Suggested Leader Responses to Student Problems

Problem	How the Leader Can Help
Mother is on drugs again, is out on the street. Student's thoughts: • "She's going to over-dose." • "She's not there to help me." Student's possible actions: • Try to get her into rehab. • Find her and ask her to stop.	*"I'm sorry that is happening. This is one of those problems that you are not going to be able to 'fix' or 'solve' easily. But let's work on it anyway and see if there are things you **can** do to try to feel better or get some control over the situation."* Possible Hot Seat thoughts that the student might be able to think of: • "She's done this before and then got herself clean. She might be able to do that again." • "I can take care of myself now, and can get help from others if I need it." Possible helpful actions that the student might put on a list: • Talk to aunt/grandmother/father and get some support. • Tell school counselor that you are having this problem. • Stay with a friend until things settle down.
The violence in the neighborhood is so bad that it is really not safe to walk to school. Student's thoughts: • "Its too dangerous." • "There is nothing I can do." Student's possible actions: • Stay home from school. • Try to get a ride from my mom (but she always says no).	*"This is a problem a lot of you are having. Let's talk about if there are any other ways to look at this situation, or anything you can do."* Possible Hot Seat thoughts that students might be able to think of: • "All the other students are in the same situation and are getting to school somehow. I can too." • "I could ask a friend to walk to school with me." Possible helpful actions that the student might put on a list: • Talk to school administration/ police/community action group to improve the situation. • Each day, arrange to walk with a friend or a group of others in the neighborhood. • Organize a "walk to school" program.

L9

Review Facing Your Fears and determine whether continued work is necessary. If so, address this individually via parent phone calls or private discussions with the students. If students are reporting low Fear Thermometer levels for most things on their lists, congratulate them and address the need to continue.

3.   Practice with Problem Solving and the Hot Seat

In this part of the lesson, most of the time is devoted to practice and review. Depending on the group, time can be devoted to problem solving, to the Hot Seat, or, in most cases, to both. Focus the group and individual members on real-life problems that are currently interfering with their lives. Use this time to consolidate techniques and help children develop skills to handle real problems.

Engagement Activity

Divide the group into two teams. Present a problem that has several people involved (see the example that follows, but try to use something relevant to the group). Assign the role of "John" to one team and the role of "Anna" to the other. First, use the Hot Seat to challenge negative thoughts for each of the roles. Then have each group follow the problem-solving steps to make a decision about what to do for each role. Compare the decisions and discuss them as a group.

Example

"John, Anna, and Diana are all meeting at the school dance on Friday night. They have been friends since elementary school. Right after they get to the dance, John and Diana want to leave to get something to eat. Anna wants to stay at the dance—there is a boy that she likes there. They tell her to stay, but she says she wants them to stay too. They still want to leave."

Assign the thoughts of John to one group, the thoughts of Anna to the other. Have each team do the Hot Seat to counteract negative thoughts leading to anger for John/Anna. Then brainstorm solutions, weigh pros and cons, and pick a solution. Convene the two teams and ask them to present both the solution and the reason they picked it. If the solutions match (i.e., if they work for both parties), it is the end of the exercise. If they do not match, have them negotiate a compromise that works for both teams.

4.   Review of Key Concepts

Structure an informal review of the key concepts the children have learned. One option is to create a trivia game and to give points for correct answers. Here are some sample questions:

- Name three common reactions to trauma.
- What is one question you can ask yourself when you have a negative thought?
- Name another way (besides asking yourself questions) to combat negative thoughts.
- What is a good thing to do if you aren't sure how to handle a problem?
- When something bad happens to us, is it better to think about it and talk about it, or to try to avoid it completely?'

5.   Plan for Independent Practice

Hand out the "Evaluation Form" and explain how it works. Explain also that the students do not have to put their names on it, but that it will be used to improve the program in the future. Ask students to be as honest as possible in evaluating the group.

6.   Review

Briefly review what happened in the group, then preview the next session.

> *"Today we got a lot of practice, and you all should feel ready to handle all those problems out there in your lives. Next time, we'll talk more about the future and what you can do to protect yourself when new stressors come up. It will be our last group together."*

L9

Lesson Ten: Planning for the Future and Graduation

1. Introduce Agenda for the Session	4. Graduation Ceremony and Individual Appreciation
2. New Group Member Game	
3. Planning for the Future	5. Wrap-up and Goodbyes

Overall Goal

Help students review and celebrate their progress and consolidate skills they have learned.

Student Objectives

1. Students will identify positive changes/progress made during the group.
2. Students will anticipate possible future challenges.
3. Students will consider ways to apply skills to future situations.
4. Students will celebrate graduation from SSET.

Materials

1. Copies of the "Note to Self" worksheet (p. 188).
2. Copies of the "Certificate of Achievement" (p. 190), signed by the group leader.
3. Special snacks, gifts, treats, and/or party supplies.
4. "Return to Class" slips (filled out).

Leader Preparation

1. Review "Ending the Group" (p. 47).
2. Review individual students' progress.
3. Have at least one genuine positive statement in mind regarding each student and/or his/her involvement in the group.
4. Plan and purchase any items necessary for the celebration (e.g., food, small toys, games, party supplies).
5. Complete and sign all copies of the "Certificate of Achievement."
6. Make phone call to parents.

Procedures/Teaching

1.   Introduce Agenda for the Session

Welcome students to the support group and briefly review what will happen in today's lesson.

"Welcome to our last group meeting. First we're going to play a game to see what you've learned. Then we are going to talk about how you might use the skills you've learned during the group to help you in future situations that may be challenging. Then I am going to hand out graduation certificates and we are going to spend some time celebrating all of the progress that each of you has made."

2.   New Group Member Game

The goal of this section is to review what was learned in the group by pretending that you (the group leader) are a new student entering the group. You will tell them a bit about yourself and the group members will suggest ways you can handle your problems.

"Let's pretend that I'm a student in this school who is joining this support group. A few months ago, my little brother got shot in a drive-by, and I'm feeling really stressed out. He's okay now, but he's still not back at school. I'm going to tell you some of my problems, and I want you all to tell me ways that I might try to feel better or try to solve the problem. You can tell me about any of the things that we've worked on in this support group. Are you ready?"

Summarize this exercise by highlighting the things that students have learned during the program.

"This shows me that you all really know a lot now about how to look after yourselves and other people. You could lend support to others that need it, but you can also help yourselves if something bad happens in the future or if you are just feeling stressed out."

3.   Planning for the Future

The goal of this part of the lesson is to consolidate the skills and anticipate the future problems of group members. Work on relapse prevention by anticipating future problems and how the children will handle them using the skills they have learned. Make sure to highlight group members' strengths as well as areas in which they should continue to practice skills. In this section, **lead a group discussion** that covers the following kinds of topics.

Engagement Activity

"Since this is your last group, let's take a few minutes to review with you how it went and what you'll do in the future. Let's talk about

- *what you got out of the group*
- *what you see as the biggest challenges you'll face in the next few months or few years*
- *how you can apply the skills you learned here to tackle those challenges*
- *how you can recognize avoidance. What are the warning signs? What can you do?"*

L10

Highlight avoidance as problematic, and make the following point:

"Avoidance can easily creep back into your life. You'll notice that you've stopped thinking about the event, stopped talking about it, stopped going certain places, stopped doing certain things [use examples from group]. It's natural to stop thinking about what happened to you gradually over time. That's part of the normal recovery process. But you might ask yourself the following questions:

- *Do I feel like I have to avoid thinking about it/talking about it?*
- *Is this avoidance getting in my way?*
- *Is it interfering with school or work or relationships?*
- *Is it stopping me from doing the kinds of things I want to do?*
- *Could I do this thing/talk about what happened if I needed to?*

"If it is getting in your way or you feel like you really couldn't do this thing/talk about what happened, use the skills you learned here to start doing all those things again until it gets easy again. You might need to work on this a few different times during your life."

Ask students to fill out the "Note to Self" worksheet based on this discussion.

*"We have one last worksheet to fill out. I want each of you to write yourself a note or reminder of what **you** can do for yourself if you are feeling stressed out in the future. Keep this note with you, someplace safe at home or in your locker, and look at it the next time you are feeling upset or stressed."*

Spend a few minutes discussing the type of future contact you will have with the group, if any (e.g., reunions, booster lessons, individual contact). Tell them how to reach you (if applicable) or how to get additional help somewhere else if they need it.

4. Graduation Ceremony and Individual Appreciation

The purpose of this part of the lesson is to provide closure to the group and give students a chance to receive positive feedback from the leader and other group members about their individual progress. If possible, present each group member with a "Certificate of Achievement," bring in food and beverages, or give students little gifts to acknowledge their accomplishments in the group. Summarize the main accomplishment for each group member in some fashion and highlight strengths.

Engagement Activity

"Since this is your last group, let's take a few minutes to review the progress you've each made. I will start off by telling each of you something I've appreciated about your participation in the group, then each of you may add positive comments for each other or the group as a whole if you'd like."

Examples

"When Jamar started group, it was really hard for him to talk about what happened. In the group, he was able to write the stories about what happened, and now he can probably talk about it to whomever he wants. That took a lot of courage."

"Carmen has been working hard on the problems with her sister. Now she knows how she wants to handle them."

Implementation tip

An alternative to having kids verbalize positive feedback for each other is to hand out slips of paper and ask each student to write down something positive about each group member or about the group as a whole. Then you may read them aloud anonymously.

---

5. Wrap-Up and Goodbyes

Briefly summarize the experience of the group, and say goodbye.

"Well, this is the end of our ten groups together. I want to tell you all how much I've enjoyed this group. I feel that we've all learned a lot from one another, and that we have given each other really valuable support. I'm going to miss this group. I know I'll continue to see you in the hallways and around the school, and I'll look forward to that. And if you are having any problems later on, I can help you talk to the school counselor or [fill in the appropriate referral mechanism]. Now that the group is over, you should think of me like any other teacher, but one who knows you pretty well and respects you a lot."

Remind the students about parent phone calls, if applicable.

Parent phone call

If you plan to make parent phone calls at the end of group, remind group members that this will occur. Use the phone call to review the group member's progress and areas that require additional work. Highlight progress and strengths to parents. Make any referrals or plans necessary to continue interventions with the parent and group member together.

LESSON MATERIALS AND WORKSHEETS

Lisa H. Jaycox
Audra K. Langley

Lesson One: Introduction

- » Confidentiality Contract
- » The Dos and Don'ts of the M&M Game
- » Why I Am Here
- » Goals
- » Letter to Parents

Confidentiality Contract

By signing my name below, I agree to keep everything that other people say during the group private and expect that other group members will do the same.

_____ _____
Signature of Group Member   Date

_____ _____
Signature of Group Member   Date

_____ _____
Signature of Group Member   Date

_____ _____
Signature of Group Member   Date

_____ _____
Signature of Group Member   Date

_____ _____
Signature of Group Member   Date

_____ _____
Signature of Group Member   Date

_____ _____
Signature of Group Member   Date

_____ _____
Signature of Group Member   Date

_____ _____
Signature of Group Member   Date

_____ _____
Signature of Group Member   Date

The Dos and Don'ts of the M&M Game

Do

- *Do* attempt to get all students to say something about themselves.
- *Do* keep questions personal but comfortable.
  - Examples: favorite sport or activity, favorite food, least favorite food, favorite movie, favorite band or singer, favorite school activity, favorite after-school activity.
- *Do* reflect students' answers without probing.
  - Examples: "Jim likes ice skating. Who else has a blue M&M?"

Don't

- *Don't* ask probing follow-up questions that would lead to longer turns or more disclosure.
  - Examples: "You like ice skating? Where do you go for that? Have you taken lessons?"
- *Don't* spend too much time on any particular group member.
- *Don't* ask overly personal questions or ones that could cause tensions.
  - Examples: questions about best friends/boyfriends/girlfriends, favorite things to do on a date.
- *Don't* react strongly if a student gives you a provocative answer. Instead, just move along to another student.
  - Example: If the leader asks "What is your favorite after-school activity," and a student says "Getting drunk," the leader says "Okay, I hope that's a joke. Who else has a blue M&M?"

Name: _____   Date: _____

Why I Am Here

In the blank space below, write in what you'd like to tell the group about what happened to you (the event that you chose to work on in the group). Remember, everyone is here because they had something bad happen to them; you are safe here in this group.

_____

_____

_____

_____

_____

_____

_____

_____

_____

_____

_____

_____

_____

_____

_____

_____

_____

_____

Name: _____   Date: _____

Goals

Please write some things about yourself that you are proud of:

_____

_____

_____

_____

Our group is designed to help you move on from a traumatic experience.

What do you want to get out of the group? (Check all that apply.)

BY THE END OF THIS GROUP . . .

I want to feel LESS:

❏ Nervous   ❏ Scared   ❏ Angry   ❏ Upset   ❏ Sad

I want to feel MORE:

❏ Happy   ❏ Calm   ❏ Excited   ❏ Relaxed

I want to change the way I do things and think about things so that I can:

❏ Calm myself down when I feel upset.

❏ Think about things that happened without feeling upset.

❏ Talk about things that happened without feeling upset.

❏ Stop avoiding things that make me nervous.

❏ Do more of the things that I used to do.

❏ Think more about things before I do them.

❏ Make better decisions.

❏ Have fewer problems with my family.

❏ Have fewer problems with my friends.

Goals—Continued

I also want to:

_____

_____

_____

_____

Parent's Section

What would you like to see changed in your child by the end of the group?

_____

_____

_____

_____

Letter to Parents

Date: _____

Dear Parents,

I want to introduce myself to you—I will be your child's Support for Students Exposed to Trauma (SSET) group leader. I am looking forward to working with your child! As you may remember, we will be working on helping your child with the following things in the groups:

- feeling calmer and being able to relax
- understanding the ways students can be affected by trauma
- coping with problems in daily life
- feeling less upset and nervous when he/she thinks about what happened.

I want to invite you tell to me about any concerns you have about your child, and to answer any questions you have. Please write anything you wish below, and tell me the best place and time to reach you by telephone.

Sincerely,

— — — — — — — — — — — — — — — — — —

Check one:

❑ I don't have any questions or concerns.

❑ Please call me to discuss:

_____

_____

_____

_____

Phone numbers: _____   Best time to call: _____

Parent signature: _____

Lesson Two: Common Reactions to Trauma and Strategies for Relaxation

» List of Problems People Have After Stress

» Information About Common Reactions to Stress or Trauma

» Activities

List of Problems People Have After Stress

Having nightmares or trouble sleeping.

Thinking about it all the time.

Wanting to NOT think or talk about it.

Avoiding places, people, or things that make you think about it.

Feeling scared for no reason.

Feeling "crazy" or out of control.

Not being able to remember parts of what happened.

Having trouble concentrating at school or at home.

Being on guard to protect your self; feeling like something bad is about to happen.

Jumping when there is a loud noise.

Feeling anger.

Feeling shame.

Feeling guilt.

Feeling sadness/grief/loss.

Feeling bad about your self.

Having physical health problems and complaints.

Name: _____ Date: _____

Information About Common Reactions to Stress or Trauma
(Handout for Parents)

Show this to your parents. Tell them which things are bothering you.

There are many different ways that young people react to stressful life events. Below we've listed several kinds of reactions, all of which are very common. We've asked your child to show this list to you and to talk with you about which ones he or she has had problems with recently. You might also notice the way that you've reacted to stressful events in your own life. Feel free to call us if you have any questions about these problems or the way in which the group will address them.

Having nightmares or trouble sleeping. When something really scary or upsetting happens, it takes a while to figure out exactly what happened and what it means. After severe stress or trauma, people tend to keep thinking about what happened in order to "digest" it, just like your stomach has to work to digest a big meal. Nightmares are one way of digesting what happened.

Thinking about it all the time. This is another way to digest what happened. Just like nightmares, thinking about the trauma all the time is a problem because it makes you feel upset. It can be unpleasant.

Wanting to NOT think or talk about it. This is natural, since it is upsetting to think about a past stress or trauma, and doing so can make you feel all sorts of emotions. Avoiding it makes things easier, but only for a little while. It's important to digest what happened sooner or later. So, while avoiding it sometimes makes sense, you have to set aside some time to digest it also.

Avoiding places, people, or things that make you think about it. Just like not want-ing to talk about or think about the trauma, avoiding situations that remind you of what happened can help you feel better right then. The problem with this, though, is that it keeps you from doing normal things that are an important part of your life.

Feeling scared for no reason. Sometimes this happens because you remember what happened to you or because you are thinking about what happened. Other times it happens because your body is so tense all the time that you just start feeling scared.

Feeling "crazy" or out of control. If a lot of these common reactions are problems for you, you can start to feel really out of control or even crazy. Don't worry, though; these problems don't mean that you are going crazy. They are all common reactions to stress or trauma.

Not being able to remember parts of what happened. This happens to a lot of people. The stressful event can be so awful that your memory doesn't work the way it usually does. Sometimes it gets easier to remember it later

Information About Common Reactions to Stress or Trauma—Continued

on, and sometimes it gets harder. This can be frustrating, but it's really normal.

Having trouble concentrating at school or at home. With all the nervousness you are feeling and all the time you are spending thinking about what happened, it can be hard to concentrate on schoolwork or even what your friends or family say to you.

Being on guard to protect yourself; feeling like something bad is about to happen. After something bad happens to you, it makes sense to be prepared for another bad thing to happen. The problem with this is that you can spend so much time waiting for the next bad thing to happen that you don't have time or energy for other things in your life. Also, it is scary to think something bad is going to happen all the time.

Jumping when there is a loud noise. This is another way to say that your body is prepared for action in case something else happens.

Feeling anger. Sometimes people feel angry about the stress or trauma that happened, or about the things that happened afterward. Other times, people just feel angry all the time, at everything and everybody.

Feeling shame. Sometimes people are ashamed about what happened to them or how they acted. Even though it's hard to believe, this gets better the more that you talk about what happened. If you keep it a secret, it's hard for the shame to go away.

Feeling guilt. People can feel guilty about what happened or about something they did or did not do. Sometimes you blame yourself for things that you couldn't control. You may also feel guilty for upsetting other people. Guilty feelings can make it hard to talk about what happened.

Feeling sadness/grief/loss. Sometimes stress events include losing someone close to you or losing something that is important to you. This makes you feel sad and down.

Feeling bad about yourself. Sometimes, all this stress can make you feel really bad about yourself, like you're a bad person or that no one likes you. This makes it harder to be friendly and to have fun with others.

Having physical health problems and complaints. Stress has an effect on your body as well. People tend to get sick more often and to notice pain and discomfort more often when they have been under stress.

Name: _____   Date: _____

Activities

Education and Relaxation

1. Did you show the "Information About Common Reactions to Stress or Trauma" handout to your parent and talk about which problems are bothering you?

    Yes—How did it go?

    _____

    _____

    _____

    No—Why not?

    _____

    _____

    _____

2. What was a good time in your house to practice your relaxation? When did you practice your relaxation?

1st time: _____   How did it go? _____

    _____

    _____

2nd time: _____   How did it go? _____

    _____

    _____

3rd time: _____   How did it go? _____

    _____

Lesson Three: Thoughts and Feelings

» Fear Thermometers
» Noticing Your Thoughts and Feelings

Fear Thermometers

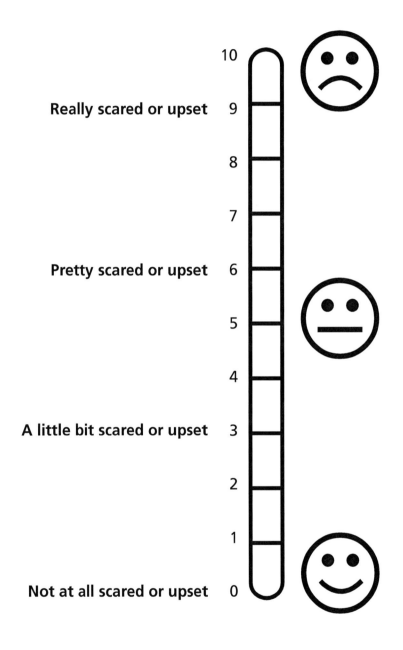

Fear Thermometers—Continued

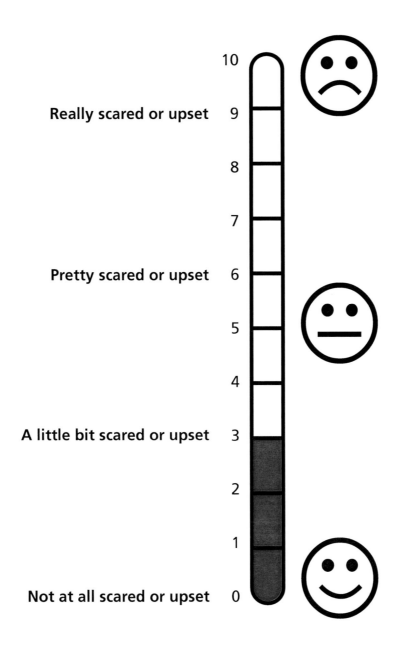

Really scared or upset

Pretty scared or upset

A little bit scared or upset

Not at all scared or upset

Fear Thermometers—Continued

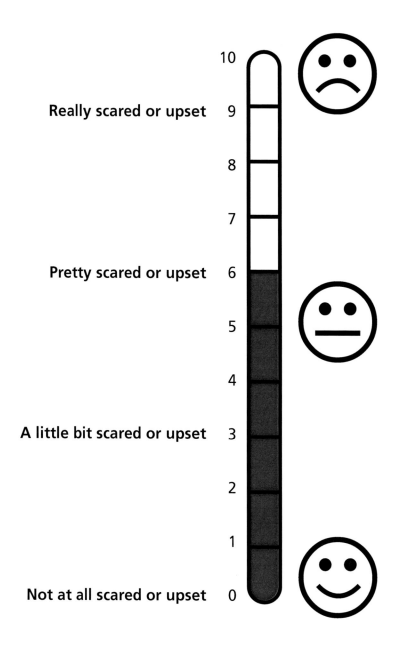

Really scared or upset 9

Pretty scared or upset 6

A little bit scared or upset 3

Not at all scared or upset 0

Fear Thermometers—Continued

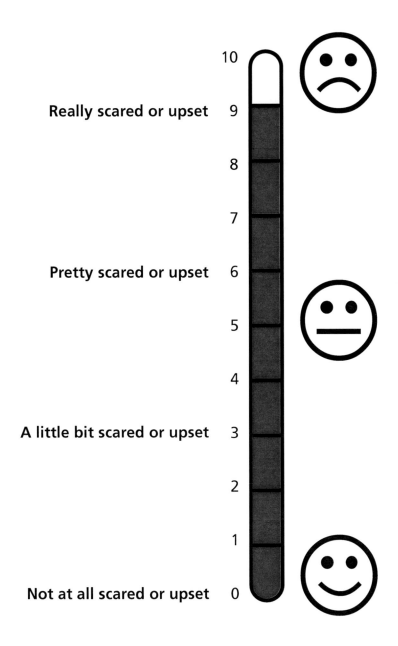

Really scared or upset   9

Pretty scared or upset   6

A little bit scared or upset   3

Not at all scared or upset   0

Name: _____   Date: _____

Noticing Your Thoughts and Feelings

What happened? Write down a situation when you felt upset, happy, sad, etc. Example: *My mother yelled at me.*	
Feelings	**Thoughts**

L3

Lesson Four: Helpful Thinking

» The Dos and Don'ts of the Hot Seat Activity

» Questions You Can Use to Argue Against Negative Thoughts

» Hot Seat Exercise

The Dos and Don'ts of the Hot Seat Activity

Do

- *Do* attempt to get all students to generate examples, negative thoughts, and questions to elicit realistic counter-thoughts, and have each student try a turn in the Hot Seat during Lesson Four.
- *Do* attempt to clarify thoughts versus feelings.
    - Example 1: Student says "I would be feeling like something bad was about to happen." Clarification: "Okay, you would be thinking that something bad was going to happen? How would you feel based on that thought?
    - Example 2: Student says "I would be thinking that I'm really mad." Clarification: "Okay, so you would be feeling really mad. What in particular would you be thinking that might be making you feel so angry?
- *Do* continually reassure students that these negative thoughts are normal and make sense given their experiences. Assure them that learning skills to challenge negative thoughts can keep those thoughts from getting in their way. But remember also that some negative thoughts are realistic or true, and we cover problem solving in Lessons Eight and Nine to help with these sorts of problems.
- *Do* probe for specific fears associated with identified feelings. (Remember to look for some of the underlying maladaptive cognitions, like "The world is a dangerous place" or "I am incompetent to handle myself.") Once you find the underlying thought, you can use the questions we teach in this lesson to challenge them effectively.
    - Example 1: Student says, "I am really scared to sleep by myself. I am always afraid something bad might happen."
      Clarification: "Okay, what in particular are you worried may happen when you are sleeping by yourself?"
      Examples of responses: "Someone may break in," "My parents might leave without me knowing," "I may have a bad dream," "I may not be able to fall asleep."
    - Example 2: Student says, " I would be feeling really embarrassed to talk in front of the class."
      Clarification: "What in particular would you be afraid might happen when you talk in front of the class?"
      Examples of responses: "I will forget what to say," "I will trip on my way up to the front."
      Further clarification: "And what are you afraid will happen then?"
      Examples of responses: "They will laugh at me/throw things at me," "They will think I'm stupid."

Don't

- *Don't* challenge realistic/adaptive thoughts. In other words, if a child's thoughts about a situation are realistic or true, we do not want to challenge them. Many of these situations may be deferred to social problem-solving skills. How can you tell if they are realistic or unrealistic?

The Dos and Don'ts of the Hot Seat Activity—Continued

To figure it out, we ask ourselves and the rest of the group the first two Hot Seat questions:

Check the facts—

> *How do I know this is true?*
> *Has this happened before?*
> *Has this happened with other people or in other situations?*

Other ways to think about it—

> *Is there another way to look at this?*
> *Is there another reason why this would happen?*

— Example: If a student says, "I feel nervous and think that my parents will fight after my mom has been drinking" or "I am afraid to walk near the park at night because there are gang members that might hurt me" and the events is indeed likely to occur, the thoughts appear to be adaptive and we don't want to challenge realistic thoughts. Social problem-solving skills (addressed in Lessons Eight and Nine) may assist the student in coming up with options for the situation.

L4

Name: _____ Date: _____

Questions You Can Use to Argue Against Negative Thoughts

Here are questions you can use to argue against negative thoughts:

Check the facts—

> *How do I know this is true?*
> *Has this happened before?*
> *Has this happened with other people or in other situations?*

Other ways to think about it—

> *Is there another way to look at this?*
> *Is there another reason why this would happen?*

What will happen next—

> *Even if this thought is true, what's the worst thing that can happen?*
> *Even if this thought is true, what's the best thing that can happen?*
> *What is the most likely thing to happen?*

Plan of attack—

> *Is there anything I can do about this?*

Name: _____   Date: _____

Hot Seat Exercise

In the top-most box, write something that happened to you that made you upset. Then write down some of the thoughts you had under "Negative Thoughts." Use the questions on the "Questions You Can Use to Argue Against Negative Thoughts" worksheet to find new ways of thinking about what happened. The example below will show you how to complete your own worksheet.

L4

What happened?
I stayed up late because I didn't want to fall asleep.

Negative Thoughts	Helpful Thoughts
If I fall asleep, I'll have nightmares.	• *I don't have nightmares every night, so I might not have them tonight* • *Nightmares aren't real, they can't hurt me.* • *I need to get some sleep for school tomorrow, even if it means I have nightmares.*
If I fall asleep, something bad will happen.	• *I'm safe in my house and my bed. My family is here to protect me.* • *If something bad happens, I'll wake up and be able to deal with it then.*
Lying down in my bed makes me feel nervous.	• *I can practice my relaxation if I feel nervous.* • *I can remind myself that I am safe.* • *It's okay to feel nervous for a little while; eventually, I'll fall asleep.*

Hot Seat Exercise—Continued

What happened?	
Negative Thoughts	**Helpful Thoughts**

L4

Lesson Five: Facing Your Fears

» Helpful Hints for Facing Fears

» Steps Toward Facing Your Fears

» Facing Your Fears Instructions

» Facing Your Fears

» Hot Seat Exercise

» Letter to Parents

Helpful Hints for Facing Fears

- To ensure the success of the Facing Your Fears assignments
  - help group members pick reasonable assignments
  - plan them in enough detail so that they know exactly what to do
  - anticipate and discuss potential problems ahead of time.
  - For instance, if a group member chooses sleeping alone with the lights off as a practice exposure, but shares a room with a sibling, you will have to help him or her plan how to accomplish this. You may find it necessary to involve parents directly in order to get their assistance and support in creating exercises for group members.

- In addition to logistical constraints, help group members anticipate negative thoughts that might interfere with the activity.
  - For instance, ask, "When you first start to do this, what negative thoughts might come into your head?" Have them develop Hot Seat thoughts in advance and write them down so that they can readily access the helpful counter-thought when needed.

- Safety is a key issue. Make sure that the group members are planning assignments that will not expose them to any real danger over and above what they experience daily.
  - For instance, pick assignments that fit into group members' existing schedules and activities. If in doubt, consult with parents about particular assignments. But beware that parents have their own trauma histories and avoidance techniques and may be overly protective because of their own fears. If this appears to be the case, reiterate the rationale for these techniques and suggest that the parent engage in the exercises with the child, if appropriate.

- The best assignments for the first week are ones that can be done repetitively (e.g., are performed at home or close to home, or are part of the group member's normal schedule) and evoke moderate but manageable anxiety (around a 4 on the Fear Thermometer). Look for these assignments, and if they aren't on the list already, add some that will make this first try a successful one.

- Be sure to reiterate the importance of the students remaining in the situation until their anxiety goes down during each trial.
  - You may notice that when you begin to assign specific activities, group members get nervous. Be sure to conduct the assignment as a collaborative process so that group members feel in control of the process. Reiterate the rationale and examples when necessary. Remind the group members that this work will make them feel better and able to do a whole range of activities.

Name: _____ Date: _____

Steps Toward Facing Your Fears

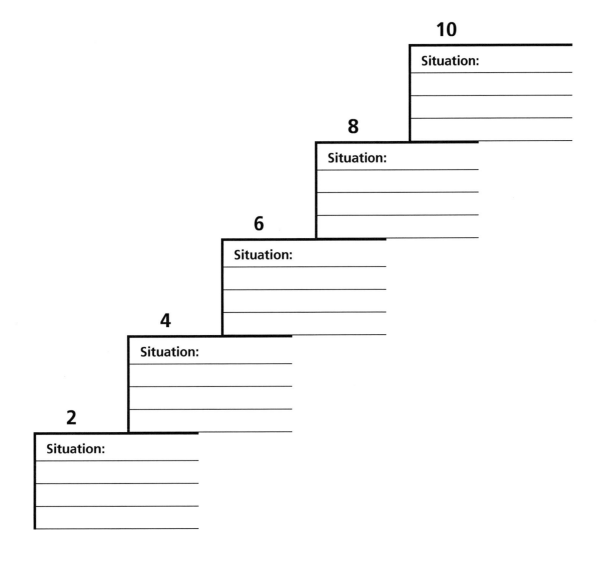

Facing Your Fears Instructions

1. Choose steps from your "Steps Toward Facing Your Fears" worksheet. Start with the bottom steps, and work your way up when you feel ready.

2. Figure out when and where you can try to do the thing you chose.
    a. You need to do it over and over again, not just once or twice.
    b. You need to be able to do it SAFELY:
        *   Don't do anything that will put you in danger.
        *   Don't do anything without telling someone first.

3. Tell a parent what you are going to do. Make sure your parent understands what you've planned and can help you with it if you need help.

4. When you do it, stick with it no matter how nervous you feel. Keep at it until you begin to feel a little bit less nervous or upset. You can use the relaxation technique if you need it. You might need to stick with it for a long time, up to an hour, before you start to feel better. If you don't feel better after an hour, make sure to try it again and again. Eventually, with enough practice, you'll start to feel more comfortable.

5. Fill out the "Facing Your Fears" worksheet and show how you felt on the Fear Thermometer before and after each time you did it. Also, write down what your highest level on the Fear Thermometer was. Talk to your group leader if you don't see any improvement.

6. If you feel very anxious, use one of the following skills to help yourself feel better:
    a. Thought Stopping
    b. Distraction
    c. Positive Imagery
    d. Relaxation.

Name: _____   Date: _____

Facing Your Fears

Write in two steps from your "Steps Toward Facing Your Fears" worksheet. Try to do each thing *five* times before the next group meeting. Each time, fill in the chart by writing both what you did and where and also your Fear Thermometer ratings before you started and after you were finished. Be sure to record the highest Fear Thermometer rating you felt while you were doing your practice. Remember to stay in the situation you've chosen until your Fear Thermometer rating goes down and the situation becomes much easier for you. Remember to use your coping strategies to help you get through!

This week, I am going to:

(1) _____

This is how I felt when I did it:

	When/where did you try it?	Fear Thermometer Ratings		
		What was your rating before you started?	What was your rating after you finished?	What was your highest rating—the worst you felt?
1st time				
2nd time				
3rd time				
4th time				
5th time				

L5

Facing Your Fears—Continued

(2) _____

This is how I felt when I did it:

	When/where did you try it?	Fear Thermometer Ratings		
		What was your rating before you started?	What was your rating after you finished?	What was your highest rating— the worst you felt?
1st time				
2nd time				
3rd time				
4th time				
5th time				

L5

Name: _____   Date: _____

Hot Seat Exercise

In the top-most box, write something that happened to you that made you upset. Then write down some of the thoughts you had under "Negative Thoughts." Use the questions on the "Questions You Can Use to Argue Against Negative Thoughts" worksheet to find new ways of thinking about what happened. Refer to the example provided in Lesson Four if you have any questions about how to complete your own worksheet.

What happened?	
Negative Thoughts	**Helpful Thoughts**

L5

Letter to Parents

Date: _____

Dear Parents,

We are about halfway through our SSET group now, and I wanted to check back in with you to see how things are going at home. The groups are going very well, and its been a pleasure to get to know your child.

We are now working on helping your child approach a situation that makes him or her feel anxious or nervous. It would be very helpful if you could review the homework from this lesson and support your child in completing it. I would also be happy to answer any questions you have about it.

In the next few weeks, we'll be asking your child to write stories about what happened to him/her. This is another place where you can be very helpful in talking to your child about what happened and supporting him or her.

Please fill in any questions or concerns that you have and I will call you to discuss them.

Sincerely,

— —

Check one:

❑ I don't have any questions or concerns.

❑ Please call me to discuss:

_____

_____

_____

_____

Phone numbers: _____ Best time to call: _____

Parent signature: _____

Lesson Six: Trauma Narrative, Part One

» Writing a Newspaper Story

» A Newspaper Picture

» Facing Your Fears

» Hot Seat Exercise

Name: _____   Date: _____

Writing a Newspaper Story

Use this worksheet to describe the trauma or stress that happened to you.

First, fill in the facts below.

Who was there? _____

_____

What happened? _____

_____

When did it happen? _____

_____

Where did it happen? _____

_____

Why did it happen? _____

_____

How did it happen? _____

_____

Now, write out a newspaper story that tell the facts you listed above:

_____

_____

_____

_____

_____

_____

Writing a Newspaper Story—Continued

_____

_____

_____

_____

_____

_____

_____

_____

_____

_____

_____

_____

_____

_____

_____

_____

_____

_____

_____

_____

_____

_____

L6

Name: _____   Date: _____

A Newspaper Picture

Now, draw a picture in the space below that goes with your newspaper story. Draw a picture of what would be in a newspaper photograph that would go with your story. Drawing a picture is another way of processing or digesting what happened to you. Don't worry about whether your drawing is "good."

Name: _____   Date: _____

Facing Your Fears

Write in two steps from your "Steps Toward Facing Your Fears" worksheet. Try to do each thing *five* times before the next group meeting. Each time, fill in the chart by writing both what you did and where and also your Fear Thermometer ratings before you started and after you were finished. Be sure to record the highest Fear Thermometer rating you felt while you were doing your practice. Remember to stay in the situation you've chosen until your Fear Thermometer rating goes down and the situation becomes much easier for you. Remember to use your coping strategies to help you get through!

This week, I am going to:

(1) _____

This is how I felt when I did it:

	When/where did you try it?	Fear Thermometer Ratings		
		What was your rating before you started?	What was your rating after you finished?	What was your highest rating— the worst you felt?
1st time				
2nd time				
3rd time				
4th time				
5th time				

L6

Facing Your Fears—Continued

(2) _____

This is how I felt when I did it:

		Fear Thermometer Ratings		
	When/where did you try it?	What was your rating before you started?	What was your rating after you finished?	What was your highest rating— the worst you felt?
1st time				
2nd time				
3rd time				
4th time				
5th time				

L6

Name: _____   Date: _____

Hot Seat Exercise

In the top-most box, write something that happened to you that made you upset. Then write down some of the thoughts you had under "Negative Thoughts." Use the questions on the "Questions You Can Use to Argue Against Negative Thoughts" worksheet to find new ways of thinking about what happened. Refer to the example provided in Lesson Four if you have any questions about how to complete your own worksheet.

What happened?	
Negative Thoughts	**Helpful Thoughts**

L6

L6

Lesson Seven: Trauma Narrative, Part Two

» Personal Story

» Personal Story Picture

» Facing Your Fears

» Hot Seat Exercise

L7

Name: _____   Date: _____

Personal Story

To plan your story, begin by answering the questions below.

When will your story begin? _____
_____

When will your story end? _____
_____

Make a list below of the things you will want to include in your story.

- Key things that happened: _____

_____

- Feelings or emotions that you had: _____

_____

- Thoughts you had: _____

_____

- Sensations or feelings in your body that you had: _____

_____

- Feelings or emotions that you had: _____

_____

What is the most important point that you want to make about what happened to you?

_____

_____

What do you want make sure that other people understand about what happened to you?

_____

_____

L7

Personal Story—Continued

Now, write out your story. Use the details above to make sure that you include everything you wanted to include.

_____

_____

_____

_____

_____

_____

_____

_____

_____

_____

_____

_____

_____

_____

_____

_____

_____

L7

Name: _____   Date: _____

Personal Story Picture

Now, draw a picture in the space below that goes with your personal story. You can draw a picture of any part of what happened. Drawing a picture is another way of processing or digesting what happened to you. Don't worry about whether your drawing is "good."

L7

Name: _____   Date: _____

Facing Your Fears

Write in two steps from your "Steps Toward Facing Your Fears" worksheet. Try to do each thing *five* times before the next group meeting. Each time, fill in the chart by writing both what you did and where and also your Fear Thermometer ratings before you started and after you were finished. Be sure to record the highest Fear Thermometer rating you felt while you were doing your practice. Remember to stay in the situation you've chosen until your Fear Thermometer rating goes down and the situation becomes much easier for you. Remember to use your coping strategies to help you get through!

This week, I am going to:

(1) _____

This is how I felt when I did it:

		Fear Thermometer Ratings		
	When/where did you try it?	What was your rating before you started?	What was your rating after you finished?	What was your highest rating—the worst you felt?
1st time				
2nd time				
3rd time				
4th time				
5th time				

L7

Facing Your Fears—Continued

(2) _____

This is how I felt when I did it:

		Fear Thermometer Ratings		
	When/where did you try it?	What was your rating before you started?	What was your rating after you finished?	What was your highest rating—the worst you felt?
1st time				
2nd time				
3rd time				
4th time				
5th time				

L7

Name:_____   Date:_____

Hot Seat Exercise

In the top-most box, write something that happened to you that made you upset. Then write down some of the thoughts you had under "Negative Thoughts." Use the questions on the "Questions You Can Use to Argue Against Negative Thoughts" worksheet to find new ways of thinking about what happened. Refer to the example provided in Lesson Four if you have any questions about how to complete your own worksheet.

What happened?	
Negative Thoughts	**Helpful Thoughts**

L7

Lesson Eight: Problem Solving

» Problem Solving

» Facing Your Fears

» Hot Seat Exercise

Name: _____   Date: _____

Problem Solving

In the first box, write about a problem that you are having. Then complete the rest of the page.

What is the problem that you will work on?

Are you having any negative thoughts about the problem? If yes, write them below.	For each negative thought, come up with a helpful thought.

Possible things you could do about the problem:

Which one of these things is best? Think about the pluses and minuses, or pros and cons, of each, and put a ★ next to the one you want to try first.

Try it! How did it work?

L8

Name: _____   Date: _____

Facing Your Fears

Write in two steps from your "Steps Toward Facing Your Fears" worksheet. Try to do each thing *five* times before the next group meeting. Each time, fill in the chart by writing both what you did and where and also your Fear Thermometer ratings before you started and after you were finished. Be sure to record the highest Fear Thermometer rating you felt while you were doing your practice. Remember to stay in the situation you've chosen until your Fear Thermometer rating goes down and the situation becomes much easier for you. Remember to use your coping strategies to help you get through!

This week, I am going to:

(1) _____

This is how I felt when I did it:

	When/where did you try it?	Fear Thermometer Ratings		
		What was your rating before you started?	What was your rating after you finished?	What was your highest rating—the worst you felt?
1st time				
2nd time				
3rd time				
4th time				
5th time				

L8

Facing Your Fears—Continued

(2) _____

This is how I felt when I did it:

| | When/where did you try it? | Fear Thermometer Ratings | | |
		What was your rating before you started?	What was your rating after you finished?	What was your highest rating—the worst you felt?
1st time				
2nd time				
3rd time				
4th time				
5th time				

L8

Name:_____   Date:_____

Hot Seat Exercise

In the top-most box, write something that happened to you that made you upset. Then write down some of the thoughts you had under "Negative Thoughts." Use the questions on the "Questions You Can Use to Argue Against Negative Thoughts" worksheet to find new ways of thinking about what happened. Refer to the example provided in Lesson Four if you have any questions about how to complete your own worksheet.

What happened?	
Negative Thoughts	**Helpful Thoughts**

L8

Lesson Nine: Practice with Social Problems and the Hot Seat

» Evaluation Form

Evaluation Form

Please fill out this form to show us what you thought about the support group. Your name will not be on the form—please be honest! Your feedback will help us improve the program in the future.

Circle how true you think each sentence is.

1. The group leader showed interest in me.

   Very true   Mostly true   A little bit true   Not at all true

2. The group leader was friendly and warm.

   Very true   Mostly true   A little bit true   Not at all true

3. The group leader listened to what I said.

   Very true   Mostly true   A little bit true   Not at all true

4. The other kids in the group listened to what I said.

   Very true   Mostly true   A little bit true   Not at all true

5. The group leader seemed to understand my problems.

   Very true   Mostly true   A little bit true   Not at all true

6. The group leader answered my questions.

   Very true   Mostly true   A little bit true   Not at all true

7. The group leader spent enough time with me.

   Very true   Mostly true   A little bit true   Not at all true

8. The group leader made me feel comfortable in the group.

   Very true   Mostly true   A little bit true   Not at all true

9. The other kids in the group made me feel comfortable.

   Very true   Mostly true   A little bit true   Not at all true

10. I got information on the kinds of problems I've been having.

   Very true   Mostly true   A little bit true   Not at all true

L9

Evaluation Form—Continued

11. I got advice on what I can do to feel better.

      Very true   Mostly true   A little bit true   Not at all true

12. The things I learned in group help me feel calmer.

      Very true   Mostly true   A little bit true   Not at all true

13. The things I learned in group help me solve problems.

      Very true   Mostly true   A little bit true   Not at all true

14. The things I learned in group help me feel better about what happened to me.

      Very true   Mostly true   A little bit true   Not at all true

15. The group helped me talk about what happened to me.

      Very true   Mostly true   A little bit true   Not at all true

16. I liked the group.

      Very true   Mostly true   A little bit true   Not at all true

17. If my friend had something happen to him/her, I'd recommend that she be in the group.

      Very true   Mostly true   A little bit true   Not at all true

Things I liked best about group: Things I didn't like about the group:

_____   _____

_____   _____

_____   _____

_____   _____

_____   _____

_____   _____

L9

Lesson Ten: Planning for the Future and Graduation

» Note to Self

» Certificate of Achievement

Note to Self

When I am feeling stressed, I can use something I practiced in the SSET group to feel better:

_____

_____

_____

_____

_____

_____

_____

_____

L10

Certificate of Achievement

The certificate found on the next page may be photocopied.

L10

★ Certificate of Achievement ★

This certificate is presented to

_____

for successful completion of the SSET Program on

_____

_____
SSET Leader